Praying Through the Bible

Volume 4: Ezra, Nehemiah, and Esther

Markus McDowell

An Imprint of Sulis International
www.sulisinternational.com

Published by Sulis Press
An imprint of Sulis International
Los Angeles and London
www.sulisinternational.com

Copyright ©2019 by Markus McDowell
First Edition

All rights reserved. No part of this publication may be reproduced in any form by any means without permission from the publisher, except for the inclusion of brief quotations in a review.

All Scripture quotations, unless otherwise noted, are from the New Revised Standard Version of the Bible, copyrighted, 1989 by the Division of Christian Education of the National Council of the Churches of Christ in the United States of America, and are used by permission. All rights reserved.

Library of Congress Control Number
ISBN (print): 978-1-946849-46-5
ISBN (eBook): 978-1-946849-47-2

Other Books in this Series

Enriching Your Prayers: How to Study the Prayers of the Bible

Praying Through the Bible: Volume 1 (Genesis–Joshua).

Praying Through the Bible: Volume 2 (Joshua–Second Kings)

Praying through the Bible: Volume 3 (First Kings–Second Chronicles)

For a free copy of the companion book

*Enriching Your Prayers:
How to Study the Prayers of the Bible.*

visit https://prayingthruthebible.com/subscribe/

Contents

Preface 1
Introduction 1
Studying the Bible 9
The Types of Prayers 17
Introduction to the Prayers in Ezra 39
Prayer and the Surprising Acts of God (Ezra 1.3) 43
Patience in Prayer and the Joy of God's Answers (Ezra 3.11) 47
Living Faithfully Under a Non-Believing State (Ezra 6.12) 51
Praying for Secular Leaders and Government (Ezra 7.27-28) 57
Prayer and Fasting Go Together (Ezra 8.21) 61
Prayer and Divorce? (Ezra 10.1-11) 67
Pure Confession—no requests, no excuses, no reasons (Ezra 9.6-15) 73
Summary of the Prayers of Ezra 79
Introduction to the Prayers in Nehemiah 81
Calling and Prayer (Neh 1.5-11) 85
Prayer and Our Responsibility to Act (Neh 2.4) 91
Is It ever Appropriate to Ask God to Curse Someone? (Neh 4.4-5) 95
Does your passion match God's will? (Neh 4.9) 101
Are you aware of how you treat those who are different? (Neh 5.12-13) 105
Praying about your past (Neh 5.19) 111

Pray Continually and Do Your Job (Neh 6.9, 14) 115

Renewing your faith through prayer and physical acts (Neh 8.6) 119

How to offer a prayer of confession, Part 1 (Neh 9.3-5). 125

How to offer a prayer of confession, Part 2 (Neh 9.6-11) 129

How to offer a prayer of confession, Part 3 (Neh 9.12-25) 135

How to offer a prayer of confession, Part 4 (Neh 9.26-31) 141

How to offer a prayer of confession, Part 5 (Neh 9.32-37) 147

Bringing Together the Past and the Present in Your Prayers (Neh 12.24) 153

Adding Joy and Physical Acts to Your Prayers (Neh 12.27, 31, 42, 46) 157

Asking God to Remember You (Neh 13.14, 22)........163

Prayers for a Distinctive Faith and Life (Neh 13.25, 28-31)..169

Summary of the Prayers in Nehemiah.......................175

The Book of Esther – no prayers, no mention of God! ... 181

Appendix Prayers by Category...................................187

Preface

The first two chapters in this book are introductory, providing some background to how I approach studying the Bible and an exploration of the types of prayers we will study in this book.

If you prefer to jump right into the devotional studies, feel free! You can always return to the introductions later if you wish, or refer to them as you read the studies.

Introduction

Many of us who pray sometimes feel that our prayers could be better. We might wish we prayed more often, or wish that the words of our prayers were better (whatever that might mean to us). Maybe we wonder if we are praying the "wrong" things. Of course, we should know that, since God is our Father, He is pleased if we talk to Him at all—even badly.

Still, many of us wish we could grown in our prayer life. Maybe it seems like our prayers have become rote, distant, or missing *something*. Often, that "something" is a lack depth, richness, or variety. We find ourselves saying the same things in the same way. Most of us were never taught how to pray—we just mimicked what we heard. So we yearn for a way to enrich our prayers and add variety and depth.

After more than twenty-five years of studying prayer, both on own and while earning degrees, I still cannot say that I understand prayer in all its richness and purpose. No one can, because prayer is, to a certain extent, a mystery. It is an ongoing conversation with the divine Creator of the Universe. That does not mean, however, that we cannot learn more about prayer grow in our practice.

Scripture is a good place to begin. There are hundreds of prayers, teachings about prayer, and mentions of prayer. As I began studying them, I found a richness and variety that I had not noticed before. I saw new possibilities for prayer in their content, structure, times, and types.

It occurred to me that, if I could study every mention of prayer in the Bible, not only would I learn a lot, but it would also enrich my own prayers. What better resource than God's word?

In 2011, I began working on a project I called "Praying Through the Bible." I been writing and speaking about prayer for many years before that, and had many hundreds of people tell me that they would like to enrich their prayer life, too. So I began the project as a blog, with the first mention of prayer in the Bible.[1] During the next few years, I worked my way through each prayer in Genesis, then Exodus, and so on. The blog gained popularity and attracted followers all over the world. Like me, many wanted to enrich their prayers. My own understanding of prayer grew through comments and emails from my readers. Many asked me for a book of these studies—something they could use for personal and group study and devotion. I edited, expanded, and revised the entries into a "devotional commentary"—a Bible study with practical application. The result was the first volume in this series, *Praying Through the Bible (Vol 1): Genesis-Joshua*, followed by a second volume the next year: *Praying Through the Bible (Vol 2): Judges-Second Samuel*, and .

---

[1] See "The Personal Name of God (Gen 4.26)," *Praying Through the Bible, Volume 1 (Genesis–Joshua)* (2015).

Introduction

The Purpose of This Book

The goal of this book is to study the prayers of the Bible and use them as models for our own prayers. Each chapter examines a passage that contains a prayer, mentions prayer, or teaches about prayer. Sometimes it is only one verse or a part of a verse; sometimes it covers many verses. I have kept together prayer passages that belong together because they are part of one scene.

Each chapter contains three parts: background, meaning, and application. As noted above, this book is a "devotional commentary," which means that its primary purpose is spiritual application. To meet that goal with care, we will seek to understand each passage within the context of its section and book. Since the Bible was written in ancient times, we will also look at the historical context when helpful. Likewise, we'll look at some cultural aspects that might help us understand that ancient culture. If relevant, we will examine the original language used or a literary technique employed. Anything that helps us understand the prayer passage is fair game.

Once we have a sound understanding of the prayer in its context, we can explore how the original readers might have read it, and how the writer might have understood it. This can help us understand what it means for us. After that, we are ready to make some suggestions about how that prayer can be used to enrich our prayers.

I have attempted to keep every chapter short, to make it easy to read one passage at a sitting, and for use as a daily devotional or a group study. Some passages need more exploration than others, of course. For those, I have divided them into two or more chapters.

How to Use This Book

I offer two suggestions for using this book. First, read the prayer passage itself at least once, and perhaps more. I have included the text of each prayer at the beginning of each chapter, but you might want to read it in a different translation (or more than one). Read it out loud. Refer to the words of the prayer as you read through the chapter. If you want even more depth in your study, read the chapter or chapters of the Bible where the prayer is located.

Second, use a prayer journal or notebook to keep track of what you learn and your practice of prayer. In some chapters, I suggest writing a prayer or specific notes. Prayer is not passive, it is part of our relationship with our Creator. Just reading about it is not enough. We need to *do* it, to practice what we learn. At the end of each chapter, there are suggestions as to how to incorporate what we learned. Of course, you are free to ignore any of these suggestions and do what works best for you. But I do encourage you to put what we study in each chapter to immediate practice.

This volume begins with the first prayer in Ezra and continues through to the last prayer in Esther. Later volumes will cover the rest of the Old and New Testa-

Introduction

ments until we reach the final prayer in the book of Revelation.

It is best to begin with the first prayer and continue in order, because we will build on what we learn as we go along. However, the book is still useful if you dip into a chapter here and there (perhaps you have an interest in a particular book of the Bible or a particular character). The book includes an appendix of prayer types if you wish to explore a specific type of prayer instead of as they appear in the biblical books. Each chapter can stand on its own, although you will miss the fuller context and previous understandings.

Most of the chapters address one type of prayer. Some contain multiple types. Practice each type after each chapter. It may seem a bit artificial to pray *only* thanksgiving prayers for a while, but doing so will immerse you in that form of prayer, and, along with the study of the prayer, you will have a good practical foundation to use it more naturally. You will find some types more comfortable than others, and that is okay—but don't forget to stretch yourself by trying them all. Pushing ourselves beyond our comfort level is how we grow.

Though I describe the prayers by types, and suggest certain practices and patterns of prayer, remember that all of this is a means to an end. As you work through this book and practice your prayers, remember that prayer is primarily about relationship, not about praying a certain way or using certain types and styles. One of my favorite stories is an old Jewish one which exemplifies this point.

There was once an illiterate cowherd who did not know how to pray, so instead, he would say to God: "Master of the Universe, you know that if you had cows, and you gave them to me to look after, I would do it for nothing, even though I take wages from everyone else. I would do it for you for nothing because I love you." A certain sage chanced upon the cowherd and heard him praying in this manner. The sage said to him, "You fool, you must not pray like that." The cowherd asked him how he should pray, and the sage set about teaching him the order of the prayers as they are found in the prayer book. After the sage went away the cowherd soon forgot what he had been taught and so he did not pray at all. He was afraid to say the usual prayer about God's cows because the sage had told him it was wrong to say such things, on the other hand he could not say what the sage had told him because it was all jumbled up in his mind. That night the sage was reprimanded in a dream and told that unless the cowherd returned to his spontaneous prayer great harm would befall the sage, for he had stolen something very precious away from God. On awakening the sage hurried back to the cowherd and asked him what he was praying. The cowherd told him that he was not praying anything since he had forgotten the prayers the sage had taught him, and he had been forbidden to tell God how he would look after his cows for nothing. The sage begged him to forget what he had told him and go back to his real prayers that he had said before ever he had met him.[2]

Prayer is different for each of us, just like the communication between any two people is different. Use the guidelines and examples in each chapter to find your own way, so that for you, like the cowherd, God will find something precious in your prayer life—not because you follow a set practice you found in this book, but because you have found a way of prayer that helps you express your prayers, not someone else's. Your prayer life will be based on what you have learned, what you have heard, and what you have been told, but you should take that and made it your own. Give it back to God as a gift. If that means, for you, telling God you will look after his cows for free while you stand dirty and unkempt in a field, so be it.

---

[2] David G. Gross and Esther R. Gross, *Jewish Wisdom: A Treasury of Proverbs, Maxims, Aphorisms, Wise Sayings, and Memorable Quotations* by (Fawcett Books, 1993).

Studying the Bible

The Bible was written thousands of years ago, over a period of about 1,200 years, in a culture that is not like ours. That gap sometimes means that we will need to explore the ancient context to avoid misunderstandings. While we might wish that "God's Word" would not need such study, it is just not so (though I do believe that the major things God wants us to know are clear). God chose to direct his Word through humans, who are fallible and limited. God also chose to have these documents *preserved* by humans. The Bible did not drop down from heaven with its words divorced from a particular time, culture, or historical setting. If God had chosen to make everything easy for a 21st century Christian to understand, then an ancient person would have found much of it baffling. It is easier for a modern person to figure out how ancient people thought and viewed the world than the other way around. So God, in His infinite wisdom, chose for the Bible to be preserved in the Ancient Near East and the Greco-Roman world, in Hebrew, Aramaic, and Greek, and with all the historical and cultural peculiarities that go along with those contexts. Sometimes we will have to do some digging to make sure we understand a passage.

But there is more. It does not take a lot of detailed study to realize that each book of the Bible has its own style and character. God did not quash the personalities and styles of the writers He chose—He allowed them to write in their own way. This should not surprise us, for God has always worked through people without making them into robots or automatons.

If we wish to understand these ancient texts, we must try to bridge the gap between that world and ours. That means learning some of the history, culture, language, and society. This may be the hardest part of studying the Bible. Even today, people who travel from the Western world to the Middle East find themselves confused (and even offended) by that culture (and the reverse is true, too). The Bible portrays a Middle Eastern culture two or three thousand years ago, and that span of time adds even more differences. The good news is that many researchers have spent centuries studying those cultures, and their work is available. In this book, it is my task to sort through it all and bring the most important elements to you, to help us all enrich our prayer lives.

Once we have contextualized a passage, there is an important question to ask about what a prayer passage teaches us. Is there a *practice* that God commands, or is it a *principle* couched in ancient cultural language? For example, some New Testament passages urge women to keep silent in public gatherings (e.g., 1 Tim 2), while others depict women speaking freely in public worship (e.g., 1 Cor 11). Some might dismiss this as an example of the Bible contradicting itself, but that is a simple and narrow view of cultures, history, and life. Just like today, there were subcultures in every part of the Empire. Just like today, there were differing situations and contexts even within a subculture. There were places in the

Studying the Bible

Roman Empire where it was considered inappropriate for women to speak in public in some circumstances; there were others where it was acceptable. So one possible interpretation is that these passages reflect different subcultures and not a particular practice we must follow. Instead, there a *principle* we should follow: "people ought to act appropriately in public assemblies." What they should or should not do depends on the culture and time. However, we could adopt a different interpretation and say, no, Timothy was writing a practice for us to follow, and God does not want women speaking in public. Paul (in 1 Corinthians) ignored that issue because he was addressing a much deeper issue about disorderliness in worship. Which one makes more sense to you? Can you think of other options? This example shows the importance of studying the Bible with humility and an awareness that we may not have all the answers.

Let's look at another example. It was the practice of the earliest Christians to meet in homes, and the New Testament implies that this is what Christians should do. Is this a practice commanded by God in a literal sense: "Christians should meet (only) in homes"? If so, many of us have violated the word of God by building church buildings for worship. Or maybe the issue is a command that "Christians should meet regularly." *Where* they met was a matter of culture, history, and necessity.

All this should lead us to realize that we must also critique ourselves. We tend to argue that something we are *already* practicing is a broad principle rather than a literal command; the rest of the passage is cultural. Or, if we practice something as a literal command, then we think that it is clear that scripture teaches it as such! In other words, it is easy to search and read Scripture to support what we already believe and practice.

What if what we "think is obvious" is incorrect? Take a look at the passage in 1 Peter 1.3-4, which commands women not to braid their hair or wear jewelry. Most of us would suggest that command was cultural. Yet could we be guilty of imposing our culture on Scripture? It is a difficult question. Sometimes, studies that contextualize can help. For example, there is good reason to think the passage was initially addressing a particular situation. In some areas of the Roman Empire, prostitutes braided their hair and wore it loose, while most married women wore hair bound up. Some Christian women, especially Greek women, may have thought that "being free in Christ" meant being free some social restraints. Perhaps the writer of the letter wanted to ensure that Christian women did not appear to be like immoral women. Another option could be this: since the Roman Empire drew strict divisions between classes and status, perhaps the writer did not think worship was a place to divide by class (which would be obvious by the clothing and adornment one wore). With these two pieces of information about the Roman Empire, we can reasonably conclude (without choosing between them) that the issue was larger than just how women dressed—there was a principle at stake rather than a specific practice.

It is not always so simple, of course, and sometimes we just do not know enough to make complete sense of a passage. However, such ambiguous passages are rare, and rarely impact a core theological or doctrinal practice. (It is also important to note that our salvation does not depend on the proper interpretation of every practice. God offers grace—not only for our sins against Him and others but also for our fair misunderstandings about church practice.)

In this study of prayers, the same questions arise. Asking those questions and studying the contexts, can tell us a lot about how to understand a prayer. I use a common, three-part method of study and interpretation. While not able to answer all questions, it usually helps reveal some cultural practices that can alert us to a possible misreading or misunderstanding. This three-part approach seeks to look "behind the text," "in the text," and "in front of the text."

Behind the text. Every story or passage of scripture has an original context. It took place at a particular time, in a particular place, within a particular social and culture setting. Knowing as much as possible about those contexts provides some sense of the meaning and purpose of a passage. That, in turn, gives us some guidelines as to what the passage could mean (or could not mean). There was an original audience for whom the text was written. For example, Paul wrote First Corinthians to the church that was located in the city of Corinth, to deal with problems and questions they had. Knowing more about ancient Corinth at that time helps us understand the letter.

In the text. Scripture is written communication, that is, it is literature. The writers chose certain phrases, words, and styles to communicate God's message. They used literary devices, such as symbolism, parallelism, or chiasmus. Just like we might in an English literature class, we can analyze those elements for better understanding. Often, a story that begins and ends with a similar phrase or event tells us something important about what is the middle of the story. Furthermore, these stories were not usually written down until long after the event. How did the *later* writer's history, culture, and purpose affect how the story was told? There are levels to the literary context.

In front of the text. This is often the most difficult approach because *we* are in front of the text. We must critique ourselves and our preconceived notions. Just as the ancient writers had a cultural and social context, so do we. As you and I read a passage of the Bible, we have our biases, expectations, and worldview that we bring to the text. In other words, we read the text through the lenses of our culture, personality, and experiences. How might that cause us to misread or misunderstand a passage? The more aware we are of our own context, the better we can avoid reading a passage in a way that might blind us to its original meaning or purpose.[1]

Pulling together all three of these methods gives us a better reading of the Bible. At a minimum, we are being

---

[1] If you want to read more about these methods, see my short book, *Let the Bible Speak: A Simple, Three-Part Method for Bible Study.*

Studying the Bible

responsible with our reading. When we take the context of God's word seriously, we honor it for what it is, as opposed to just reading it for what *I* think it mans, as if the only meaning it has is what I give it. Even if this approach does not give us answers, it can make us aware of problem areas, so we will not be too dogmatic and judgmental of a different understanding. Almost always, though, these methods make the passage come alive and the message clear.

Once we have finished the three-part approach, and have a decent understanding of the prayer and its context, we ask ourselves "what does this prayer teach me?" How can you use it in your world, your context, and your life?

This approach reveals the richness of the prayer passages in the Bible, which, in turn, serves the purpose of this book: to enrich our prayer lives.

The Types of Prayers

In this book, I divide prayers into nine types (or categories). By "type" I mean the content and the purpose of the prayer. The types, as I define them, are the following:

1. Praise
2. Thanksgiving
3. Petitions
4. Intercessions
5. Prayers of Confession and Repentance
6. Laments
7. Prayer-Vows
8. Blessings
9. Curses

Some of these types will be found together in one prayer, but more often than not (and perhaps surprisingly) most prayers are of one type. Some occur more frequently than others. The Psalms contain every type—not surprising since the Psalms is a book of prayer-hymns.

Most of us tend to use only a few of these types, the most common being petition, intercession, and thanksgiving. Studying *all* of the types, and learning their purpose and how to use them, will help us have a more consistent, rich, engaging, and effective prayer life.

Each type has its unique value and purpose so that we will examine each one on its own. We should not forget, however, that these kinds of prayers are connected and can be combined. For example, in the book of Exodus, some types repeat in a clear pattern. Suffering (slavery) leads the Israelites to offer a *petition*; the petition leads to an answer from God (choosing Moses as a leader), but also brings further difficulties (the Egyptians make the Israelites suffer). The sufferings cause the Israelites to offer more *petitions*, *intercessions*, and *vows*, and that results in God delivering the Israelites from the Egyptians. The deliverance leads the people to offer prayers of *praise* and *thanksgiving*.

As we study each prayer type, remember that the flow of the prayers is important, too. If we petition God for deliverance and then neglect to praise or thank Him, we have missed part of the rich connectedness of prayer types. God desires a relationship that does not place us in the role of a child who takes without thanks, nor that of a spouse who always cries out for help but never shows gratitude. It is a relationship that ebbs and flows, gives and takes, cries and comforts, declares and responds.

The Types of Prayers

Prayers of Praise

A "prayer of praise" is a prayer that focuses on the character of God. It is not a prayer that thanks God for something, although thanksgiving prayers and prayers of praise are connected. Some might suggest this is too fine a distinction, but there is value in considering the two types as separate, even if they often overlap in practice. Consider this: while a thanksgiving prayer offers thanks to God for something He has done, a prayer of praise honors God because of who He is as Creator, the One who sustains us, and the One who loves us with perfection. Praise is about the recognition of God's being and character, rather than thanking Him for something he did.

Think of a famous person from history, someone you respect and admire above others. Let's leave Jesus out of this exercise—think of a regular human. Maybe it is a president, a king, a sports figure, a scientist, or an artist. You might, at first, be more in awe of who they are, rather than being thankful for something they did. The respect or awe that you feel is because of their character and being—their legacy, so to speak. The awe you experience is similar to the reason for a prayer of praise.

It may be difficult for us to offer pure prayers of praise. Most of us are pretty good at thanksgiving—we receive something good from someone, we thank the person. But the Bible contains plenty of models of praise-prayers for us to study and mimic. The opening chapters of Revelation provide a good example. Chapters 2 and 3 depict a pretty sad scene among the churches in Asia minor. They are poor, they have forgotten their way, pagan culture has influenced them, or they are selfish. A faithful Christian might feel quite disheartened. Chapter 4 is a scene that takes place in heaven. God is on His throne, surrounded by twenty-four elders and all manner of creatures; all are praising God. In such a dismal state of affairs on earth and in the church, they praise God because they know that He is *always* on the throne, He is always in control, He is *always* sovereign. We offer prayers of praise to God because He is in His holy temple; because He has the Final Word. We offer prayers of praise because *we* know how this story ends, regardless of how bad everything might be now.

When my children were young, we visited many of the ancient church cathedrals in Europe. My daughter, who was seven years old, did not like going inside those massive edifices. My wife and I thought that it was because of the crypts and grave markers inside. My mother had recently died, so we assumed the reminders of death made her think of her beloved grandmother. Once, on a trip to France, we visited the famous cathedral in Strasbourg, and I decided to have a serious conversation with her about her fears. As we walked down the center aisle towards the massive transept, I held her hand and asked why she was so scared of cathedrals. She stopped and leaned into me, looked up with wide eyes and said, "Because they make me feel *so* small. It scares me. I feel *this* big—" and she held out a thumb and forefinger close together.

I knelt down put my arms around her. "Yes, they *do* make us feel quite small, don't they?" I said. "But you know what? They built them that way *on purpose*. They designed them to be so big and to seem to reach to heaven, to help us remember how powerful and *awe*-some *God* is. And yet, despite all that scary power, we can still come to Him, and be with Him, just like we can be in this cathedral: because He loves us."

A look of wonder came into her eyes and she cocked her head to the side. "Really?" From that moment, she enjoyed visiting cathedrals. She lit candles for her grandmother in their chapels and touched the foot St. Peter's statue in Rome. She came to understand that the feeling of *smallness* was appropriate before God, for it reminds us of His power and His love.

That is why we offer prayers of praise.

Thanksgiving Prayers

Thanksgivings occur throughout Scripture. The basic words for "thanksgiving" appear 140 times in the Old Testament and 53 times in the New Testament. Paul's letters are full of thanksgiving prayers. Jesus gives thanks for people, for the fact that God hears him, and before meals. In the Revelation to John, elders, multitudes, and beasts offer thanksgiving to God twenty-four hours a day. In each of those instances, they thank God for something He has done for them—as an individual or as a group. Sometimes, though, thanksgivings are offered when they seem to make no sense. For example, the prophet Habakkuk stands on the walls of his city and sees disaster coming as an enemy bears down on Israel.[1] Yet he says, "Even so, I shall exult in the Lord and give thanks to the God of my salvation." (Note the combination of praise and thanksgiving in his prayer.) He praises him for who God is, then he thanks him because He is the God of his salvation.

Sometimes, thanksgiving prayers are inappropriate. For example, Jesus tells a parable of a religious leader who goes up to the Temple to pray. He sees a tax collector—people who worked for the Roman oppressors and got rich off their own people—and he thanks God that he is not like him or other "undesirables." Jesus criticizes this sort of thanksgiving.

Thanksgivings are structured in many ways; they can be long or short, they can be spontaneous or well-planned. For this study, I define a thanksgiving as a prayer which thanks God for something specific that He has done—usually for the one who is praying, or for his or her community. It can also be a thanksgiving for what God did for someone else, following after requests by the one offering the prayer. In that case, the person thanks God for answering a intercession was offered for someone else.

As with all prayers, thanksgivings are relational. They are part of the give-and-take of an ongoing conversation with God. Just like human relationships, thanksgivings can include understanding and misunderstanding, conversation and silence, joy and pain.

---

[1] Habakkuk 3.16–17.

Thankfulness is part of any genuine relationship, but it is not all of it. Thanksgiving prayers do not stand alone. They are connected with the prayers that came before: petition, vows, confession, repentance, and requests for forgiveness. In this case, a thanksgiving prayer is the response of gratitude. Still, we might offer a thanksgiving prayer merely *because* God allows us to have a relationship with Him, much like we might say "thanks for loving me" to a spouse or friend. It also means that we can offer a thanksgiving in the midst of struggles, like Habakkuk, just as we might say, "thank you for being here and comforting me" to a friend who visits us. Thanksgivings might be the most connected of all the prayer types because of the variety of situations in which it can be offered. While a petition, vow, or confession are usually offered in particular occasions, a thanksgiving prayer is always appropriate. This is why Paul tells the Thessalonian church to "give thanks in all circumstances; for this is the will of God in Christ Jesus for you."

Petitions and Intercessions

Petitions and intercessions are both common in Scripture. Both share the characteristic of asking God for something: they are both requests made of Him.

A petition is a prayer that asks for something for the one who is praying. It is a personal request. "God, please help me be generous today" is a petition. It might seem selfish to ask things for ourselves, yet it is part of a genuine relationship. Children ask their parents for things, and it is a sign of reliance. Of course, over-reliance becomes a sign of selfishness. Someone who is always asking for something does not experience a genuine richness of a relationship. But in connection with other types of prayer, petition is an appropriate part of the give and take.

An intercession, or intercessory prayer, is one which asks for something for someone else. I might pray that my wife has a good day. You might pray that a friend has successful heart surgery. We might pray that a missionary group is safe and effective. Praying on behalf of someone reflects that, as believers, our relationships are both vertical and horizontal. We pray *to* God the Father as our sustainer and redeemer, we pray *for* someone else as a loved one, fellow believer, or fellow human.

Both types of prayers are frequently found in scripture, though not as frequently as prayers of praise. We might find this surprising because most of us tend to ask for things far more often than we offer praise, thanks, confession, or repentance. This may be why we are sometimes dissatisfied with our prayers: we are missing the richness of a genuine relationship because we focus on only one or two types of prayer.

Why does Scripture suggest that prayers of intercession and petition should not be the most common types offered? The answer is, as noted above, that we need a relationship with God. But there is more to it than that. God first desired a relationship *with us*. He created us, He continues to create us, and He makes it possible for us to know Him. If petition and intercession stand alone, we turn God into a divine Santa Claus or a personal counselor. Scripture does not portray God in such a way. Instead, He is described as a father, mother, savior, creator, king, nurturer, and sustainer. Therefore, petitions and intercessions are only *part* of an ongoing relationship. If we use them alone, they are an insult to God and the relationship. Imagine if your child, spouse, sibling, or friends never thanked you, praised you, or said they were sorry. What if, most of the time, they only asked you to give them things? It would not be much of a relationship. In fact, it is not a genuine relationship at all.

Petitions and intercessions show our dependence on God and are appropriate within a full relationship. Because we praise, thanks, confess, and vow—we can also ask.

Confessions and Prayers of Repentance

Confession and prayers of repentance, like the other types, are actions that are part of a genuine relationship. In fact, confessing and repenting may be the most intimate form of communication. There would be no need for confession and repentance if we did not fail our created purpose and damage our relationships with God and others.

Confession is not something we are prone to do. We do not want to confess our misdeeds; we want to explain them. We might say: "I was afraid" or "he provoked me beyond my limits." Those excuses might be true. But confession and repentance do not address the *reason* behind a sin; they speak to the *fact* of sin and the consequential damage.

Confession and repentance are about admitting our misdeeds and pledging to do better. "I am sorry I hurt you, and I promise I will never do/say that again." We often want to add "but…" to an apology. However, true confession rejects explanation or rationalization. If we try to offer defenses and reasons, we soil the process. Instead, confession should be a declaration; repentance is a pledge to be better.

Confession and repentance are linked, but they are different. Confession is the first part: I declare my sin before God, my spouse, family, friends, and/or congregation. When we name the sin, it begins to lose its power over us. Turn on the light, and shadows become common and ordinary. "It is not a goblin's head; it is my basketball!" "It is not a gnarled old man with a knife; it is the way the shadow of a tree shines against the curtains!" When we move our sin from *inside* of us to *outside* of us, we begin to allow God to deal with it appropriately. Likewise, once it is out, it is harder to put it back (that is, to continue it). Once you have told someone of your sin, it is more difficult to ignore or rationalize it. You are held accountable—and accountability is crucial for the connected prayer type of repentance.

Repentance comes from an old Anglo-Norman/Old French word meaning "to renounce (something)," "to cease (to do something)," "to express contrition or regret." After confessing, we express our regret for the damage or hurt we have caused, and reject that behavior. A prayer of repentance disavows the act. "That is not who I am; it is not who I should be, and I reject it; I am now on a new path to avoid it in the future because I see it for what it is." A prayer of confession without repentance, or repentance without confession, would be incomplete.

The Bible is full of confessions and prayers of repentance. In much of the Old Testament, they are connected with sin sacrifices. Leviticus and Numbers both describe how they are to be offered to be cleansed of sin and forgiven.[2] These actions of sacrifice emphasize that one must confess sins to be forgiven for them. Jesus emphasizes the same thing in the Lord's Prayer.[3] During the conquest of Canaan, when the people failed to follow God's commands, tragedy fell upon them. Joshua went to the leader of the rebellious group and told him he must confess to God.[4]

Sometimes leaders confess the sins of a group of people to God, even though it may be that the leader himself did not sin. Ezra confessed the sins of his people for not separating themselves from nonbelievers, as God had asked them to do.[5] Nehemiah offers similar prayers for his people.[6] In Nehemiah 9.3, the people themselves confess their sins together as a group. Today, congregations and groups of believers rarely en-

---

[2] For instance, see Lev 5.5; 16.21; 26.40; Num 5.7.
[3] See Matt 6.12.
[4] Josh 7.19.
[5] Ezra 9-10.
[6] New 9-10.

gage in public and group confession, despite the numerous examples in the Bible. This is probably a testament to the difficulty of admitting we are wrong. While some of us might confess in private at times, or (more rarely) in public, it is not often do we hear leaders take on the sin of their congregation or a group and confess on their behalf as their leader.

If you do not know how to pray a confession, the Psalms are a good resource. Often, the words can be recited with little or no change to fit your circumstances. For example, Psalm 38.18 is an excellent beginning for a prayer of confession:

I confess my iniquity;
I am sorry for my sin.

It is a simple declaration of confession followed by a simple statement of repentance. A more complex prayer is David's prayer of confession after his affair with Bathsheba.[7] The structure of the confession is a good template for our prayers:

1. Request for mercy (51.1–2)

2. Confession of the sin (51.3)

3. An acknowledgment that the sin hurts God and others and God would be justified in punishing (51.4–5)

4. An expression of knowledge that only God can forgive and cleanse (51.6–12)

---

[7] Ps 51; read the story in 2 Samuel 11-12.

5. A look to the future (repentance) (51.13–18)
6. A statement of knowledge that God wants sincere and humble followers (51.18–19).

When we sin, we can always be forgiven and start anew—otherwise, our sins would continue to build up, burying us under the weight of failure and guilt and separating us from God. This was the reason for daily, monthly, and yearly sacrifices described and commanded in the Old Testament. For Christians, there is no need to offer those oil, grain, or animal sacrifices, because of the sacrifice of His Son, made by God, took the place of those sacrifices. That perfect sacrifice was more horrific than any animal sacrifice, but also more effective because it was God's sacrifice.[8] It need be done only once. Then, in confession and repentance, we take part in that sacrifice. Jesus becomes *our* offering for *our* sins of his own free will, and we are cleansed and forgiven.

In prayers of confession and repentance, we throw ourselves upon God's mercy, acknowledging that He is our only hope to begin again. We make a statement about our future, and we commit to being renewed, to live differently, and to serve Him. Such prayers offer us the opportunity to offer ourselves in humility and to be lifted up by the Judge himself, who says, "go, my child; you are no longer guilty. The sacrifice of sin has been

---

[8] Some people are outraged that the Jewish religion slaughtered thousands of animals a year for their own sins, but often those same people are not outraged that a man was slaughtered for their sin. We should be shamed that it was necessary, and grateful that it was offered.

paid. You are a forgiven and sinless being—now go out and live like it."

Prayers of Lament

A lament is a prayer that cries out to God in pain and loss. It does not ask God for anything (though a petition often follows a lament). Imagine a small child who is in pain and cannot fathom what is happening to them. The child cries out to their parent because the parent is the caregiver, the authority, and the nurturer. The child may even wonder why the parent is allowing the pain, though the parent may be unable to stop it—perhaps it is an illness, or an inoculation, or a cut on the arm.

For that reason, offering a lament may be the most open of prayers, because laments are an emotional cry. Laments in the Bible sometimes even question God, or call Him to account! In a time of seemingly meaningless suffering, a lament may come to the lips of a believer almost unbidden: "why, God?!"

You may have heard that one should never question, criticize, or be angry at God. This ignores the richness of prayers of lament we find in the Bible. A lament is God's way of allowing us to be honest with Him and express, with pure emotion, how we feel. Like confession and repentance, lament is deeply relational. After all, if a relationship forbids certain discussions, then it is a limited relationship. There is nothing improper about a lament, because one is *still* turning to God, like a child crying out to a parent. For this reason, laments often end with petitions, and sometimes with thanksgivings or praises. This does not mean that God always makes clear the reasons for the suffering. Yet those who pray laments in the Bible find comfort in the presence of God, even if relief does not come, just like a baby finds comfort in its mother's arms, even if the pain does not go away.

There are a few laments in the early books of the Old Testament. Hagar cries out when she and her son are banished to the desert to die.[9] Joshua and the leaders of Israel lament when they inexplicably lose a devastating battle.[10] Laments are found most often in the Psalms and in the Prophets, especially those written during the time of Exile.[11] The New Testament is not without laments, though they are rare because of the number of letters or epistles rather than stories. One of the most famous is from Jesus, while on the cross, quoting a Psalm of lament (Ps 22):

> *My God, my God, why have you forsaken me?*
> *Why are you so far from helping me, from the words of my groaning?*
> *O my God, I cry by day, but you do not answer;*
> *and by night, but find no rest.*

---

[9] Gen 21.16. See "Hagar's Lament and Petition (Gen 21.16)" in *Praying Through the Bible, Volume 1 (Genesis–Joshua)* (2015).

[10] Joshua 7.7–9. See "A Lament (Joshua 7.7–9)" in *Praying Through the Bible, Volume 1 (Genesis–Joshua)* (2015).

[11] For example, see Psalms 17:13–14; 35:4–6, 26; 44; 58:7–10; 137 (more than 20% of the Psalms are laments). The entire book of Lamentations is a highly developed lament-prayer.

> *Yet you are holy,*
> *enthroned on the praises of Israel.*
> *In you our ancestors trusted;*
> *they trusted, and you delivered them.*
> *To you they cried, and were saved;*
> *in you they trusted, and were not put to shame.*

Jesus uttered other laments as well over two cities and Jerusalem.[12]

The Psalms include both individual laments and community laments: a lament can be offered by a congregation or other group of believers in a time of tragedy, suffering, and loss. A lament is a good example of the relational nature of prayer and is a type that can add some meaningful richness to our prayer life.

Prayer-Vows

Prayer-vows, like laments, are relatively uncommon today, at least in the modern Western world. Yet they are prevalent in scripture. Perhaps this is a form of prayer that we should revive as a way to add richness to our prayers. You can judge for yourself after you have studied some them later in this book.

Vows offered to a deity were quite common in the ancient world among all people and religions. A prayer-vow is a conditional agreement with a god or goddess.

---

[12] Matthew 11:20–23 (cf. Luke 10:13ff); Matt 23:37–38 (Luke 13.34–35).

The Types of Prayers

The offerer promised to give a sacrifice or a gift of some sort, in return for the god or goddess doing something for them. For example, in 296 BC, the Roman consul Appius Claudius Caecus prayed that, if his patron goddess Bellona would give him victory in battle, he would build a temple in her name.[13]

The Old and New Testament both contain prayer-vows of a similar nature. Sometimes the offerer promises something to God and asks nothing in return. For example, a Nazarite vow is one in which a person promises not to cut the hair, drink wine, or be around unclean things for thirty days.[14] John the Baptizer took this vow, as did Paul.[15] Samson is one of the most well-known examples of a man taking a Nazarite vow, though this vow was for his entire life rather than just thirty days. These one-sided vows, where God is not asked for anything, are vows of dedication—dedicating oneself to God in some particular way for a particular time.

The second type of vows are conditional agreements with God, and are common in the Bible, too. The offeror promises to give something to God, or His work in the world, if He grants their petition. For example, Hannah vows that if God allows her to give birth to a son, she will dedicate him to the service of God.[16]

---

[13] Ovid, *Fasti*, vi.201–205. The Temple was built several years later in Rome, and dedicated on June 3, 296 BC.

[14] The full description and requirements of the vow is found in Number 6.1–21.

[15] Luke 1.15; Act 18.18, respectively.

[16] 1 Samuel 1.11–17.

Since these vows are pledges to do something *if* God does something in the future, we might wonder if they are self-serving. While a prayer-vow could be misused in that way, a genuine prayer-vow is part of the relationship between God and us. It is a give-and-take, a promise to each another, and a way of showing loyalty. We are not telling God that he *must* do something; just that if He does, we will thank Him by offering a special gift in place of a usual thanksgiving. It might be money, time, or some other benefit to God and His mission.

Two-sided vows are serious business. Psalm 66 cautions that, if you dare to offer such a vow, you had better keep it. One should think carefully and responsibly *before* offering a prayer-vow. Jephthah offered one rashly in Judges 11, with tragic results when he found out his vow meant he had to do something he had not foreseen.[17] Vows of this type should be treated with care.

The one-sided prayer-vow is an opportunity for us to show our dedication to God and a way for us to hold ourselves accountable to Him. We might vow to pray three times a day for the next month, or refrain from

---

[17] Some question whether he should have kept the vow, since it involved the sacrifice of his daughter; or whether this was an example of Israel's fall from God in offering human sacrifices. We will examine his vow in the next volume, "Rash Vows (Judg 11.30-31)." (There is a later writing that describes the daughter's long lament: Pseudo-Philo, *Liber Antiquitatem Biblicarum* 40.5–7. If you are interested in a technical discussion of the prayer, see my analysis in Markus McDowell, *Prayers of Jewish Women: Studies of Patterns of Prayer in the Second Temple Period*, 100–104.)

critical words for a day, or to skip lunch for a week and spend that time in study and prayer.

To summarize, a prayer-vow is a type of prayer that is used to hold ourselves accountable to God, dedicate ourselves to God, and expand our possibilities of prayer.

Blessings and Curses

Blessings and curses appear in Scripture as separate prayers but usually appear together. The reason for this is because they are a particular kind of petition. They do not ask God for something as much as wish it or hope for it, usually in the presence of another person or in public.

A blessing asks that good will come upon someone, that they will receive a gift, or that seeks the best for them. Curses do the opposite: they ask that punishment or harm may come upon someone. In this way, they are petitions that God do something, though they often do not ask God directly for the blessing. For example, Naomi says to her daughter-in-law, "May you be blessed by the LORD, my daughter" (Ruth 3.10).[18] Noah says, "Cursed be Canaan, the lowest slaves shall he be to his brothers" (Gen 9.25).[19] There is an element of "hope" rather than a direct request.

---

[18] See "A Blessing for a Saint (Ruth 3.10)."
[19] See "Noah's Blessings and Curses (Gen 9.25-27)" in *Praying Through the Bible, Volume 1 (Genesis–Joshua)* (2015).

I use the word "hope," yet prayer-blessings and prayer-curses are stronger than a mere "I hope this happens." In the ancient world, blessings and curses (especially the latter) were thought to have an almost magical power. If one said them correctly, in the right circumstances, they would happen. The understanding of curses and blessings in the Old and New Testament is rarely, if ever, presented in that "magical sense." Still, they have more power than just "I hope God brings justice upon you." Prayer-blessings and prayer-curses attest to a strong belief in the spoken word and the ear of God.

Blessings are pronounced upon individuals, groups, or nations. Leaders and priests utter them; ordinary people speak them. Blessings can be pronounced upon God (and often are). In the latter, the blessing almost becomes a kind of praise/thanksgiving/blessing; that good should come to God because He deserves it.

Non-believers in the Bible sometimes offer blessings. Melchizedek blessed Abram (Gen 14.19-20); [20] King Hiram blessed Solomon (1 Kings 5.7); the Queen of Sheba blessed the God of Israel (1 Kings 10.6). Blessings can be for something specific or merely a general pronouncement of good. They can be formal or informal, spontaneous or traditional.

Jacob (Israel) blesses his grandsons in a traditional "deathbed" pronouncement upon children (Gen 48.15–

---

[20] See "Melchizedek Blesses Abram (Gen 14.19-20) in *Praying Through the Bible, Volume 1 (Genesis–Joshua)* (2015).

The Types of Prayers

20). [21] The priest Levi blessed all the people of Israel (Lev 9.22). [22] The book of Ruth is filled with prayer-blessings upon a number of people. In the New Testament, Elizabeth blesses Mary (Luke 1.42, 45); Jesus blesses children (Mark 10:16) [23] and offers blessings at meals (Luke 9.16). Paul's letters are filled with teaching about blessings, blessings on God, and blessings on his readers. [24]

Curses, likewise, can be general or specific, formal or spontaneous. In scripture, they are usually the result of some evil done by a person or a warning of what will come if someone does something forbidden. Joshua curses anyone who might try to rebuild Jericho (Josh 6.26);[25] Jeremiah curses the day of his birth and the person who announced it (Jer 20.14–18). We might think the New Testament would be sparse with curses, but there are plenty. Peter offers a curse when he denies that he is one of Jesus' followers (Mark 14.71);[26] Paul pronounces a curse on anyone who preaches a different gospel than the one he taught (Gal 1.9).

As noted, blessings and curses often appear together, in a formula style: "if *this* then a blessing, if *that* then a

---

[21] See "Israel blesses the Sons of Joseph (Gen 48.15-16, 20)" in *Praying Through the Bible, Volume 1 (Genesis–Joshua)* (2015).

[22] See "Aaron Blessing the People (Lev 9.22) in *Praying Through the Bible, Volume 1 (Genesis–Joshua)* (2015).

[23] See the parallels in Matt 19.15 and Luke 18.17.

[24] See, for example, Romans 12.14; 1 or 7.40; 2 Cor 1.3; Eph 1.3.

[25] See "A Curse-Prayer (Joshua 6.26)" in *Praying Through the Bible, Volume 1 (Genesis–Joshua)* (2015).

[26] He does it twice in Matthew 26.72, 74.

curse." Noah blesses two of his sons but pronounces a curse on the third because of his shameful actions against his father (Gen 9.25–27).[27] Jesus offers four blessings and then contrasts it with four curses or "woes" (Luke 6:20–26). The book of Revelation contains many blessings and curses—a whole series of them are found in Revelation 22.7–18.

These examples of prayer-blessings and prayer-curses show us that they can enrich our prayer lives. It is likely that most of us do not think too deeply about blessings, only offering them before meals, weddings, and other particular occasions. Yet blessings can play a larger role in our lives, as we will see in this book. Curses are more difficult—many of us might think that God would not want us to curse anyone. Curses can be misused: Rebekah places a curse on herself to help her son deceive his father (Gen 27.12–13).[28] Abner pronounced a self-serving curse (2 Sam 3.9). In the New Testament, Paul wrote: "bless and do not curse" (Rom 12.14). But he is writing only to those who are persecuting his readers. How can curses be used correctly in a modern Christian life?

The best way is to learn about them in context. We will read a few of them in this book, and you can decide for yourself the most responsible way to use them.

---

[27] See "Noah's Blessings and Curses (Gen 9.25-27)" in *Praying Through the Bible, Volume 1 (Genesis–Joshua)* (2015).

[28] See "A Blessing Wrought in Deception (Gen 27.7, 12–13, 27–29; 28.2-4)" in *Praying Through the Bible, Volume 1 (Genesis–Joshua)* (2015).

Introduction to the Prayers in Ezra

The person of Ezra, along with Nehemiah, are two of the greatest men in Israelite history. They are both credited with being key figures in bringing the Jews back from Exile and creating a new community wrought from the destruction of the Temple and their lands. The prayers in the book of Ezra offer us an opportunity to learn about prayers of confession.

Contents

The books of Ezra and Nehemiah were originally one book, but were separated into two in the 3d century AD by the theologians Origen and Jerome.

After the description of Judah, the Israelite leaders were taken into exile to Babylon. For eighty years they lived there, and spend much of the time reassessing how this tragedy had happened. Was the Babylonian god more powerful than YHWH? Did God no longer care about them? Some believed those things. But many of the priests and scholars began to review the writings of their ancestors: from Genesis to 2 Chronicles. And they discovered that God had been long-suffering, patient, and gracious to them, while they had continually failed to be faithful. They rethought their faith and began a renewed focus on what it meant to be God's people: it was not enough for the king and the priests to follow—everyone should be faithful. It was these people who edited and preserved the biblical writings, with a new focus on scripture, and on what it meant to follow God.

After a time, the Babylonian Empire was defeated by the Persians. Ezra begins by describing how the king of Persia, Cyrus, allowed the Jews to return to their land under a leader named Sheshbazzar. There, he oversaw the rebuilding and reconstruction of the Temple. The people had to deal with opposition from people who had remained behind, but the project was eventually completed.

Ezra came next, sent by King Artaxerxes, bringing more exiles back to Jerusalem. There, he dealt with some of the problems he found in the unfaithfulness of the people.

Themes

While the books are primarily historical in their structure and content, there are a few themes that appear throughout both works.

1. God kept his promise to eventually restore his people from exile to their land. He did this by working through Persian kings and Jewish prophets.

2. Opposition to God's people and their renewal was fierce at times, but God was faithful to his people, and they prevailed.

3. Humility and humbleness were required—Israel had been an unfaithful people for much of their history, and in need of constant correction. They now awaited a "new covenant" that the prophets had promised (See Jeremiah 31, Joel 1, Ezekiel 36).

4. "All Israel" was restored. This does not mean political sovereignty; it refers to the temple, worship, and sacrifices, and the keeping of the law of Moses.

The Prayers

There are seven mentions of prayer in the book of Ezra. The prayers, as usual, reflect the themes above. As we might expect, the first three are praises or thanksgiving—thanks that God has begun restoring his people to their lands. There are a couple of petitions, and the rest are confessions, both private and public, mirroring the need for the people to confess their sins and renew their faith and devotion to God.

While we probably spend most of our time offering prayers of praise, thanksgiving, and petitions or intercessions, the setting and situation of Ezra allow us to focus more on prayers of confession than other books.

Prayer and the Surprising Acts of God (Ezra 1.3)

Any of those among you who are of his people—may their God be with them!—are now permitted to go up to Jerusalem in Judah, and rebuild the house of the LORD, the God of Israel—he is the God who is in Jerusalem...

Background

The book of Ezra opens with a proclamation from the King of Persia, Cyrus. The first words of the book tell us that it was Cyrus' first year as king, and that God caused Cyrus to issue this proclamation throughout the land. The proclamation says that any Jews who are still alive in his lands may now go to Jerusalem and rebuild the Temple.

The author then tells us that the heads of the families of Judah and Benjamin—those whose ancestors were taken away into Exile eighty years before, prepared to go.

Their neighbors (both Jews who had decided to stay, as well as non-Jews), donated to their cause. King Cyrus also had all the furnishings returned to them that had been taken from the Temple by the Babylonians.

Meaning

The ancient Empire of Assyria had attacked and destroyed northern Israel, taking away all the people and scattering them among the Empire. Later, the Babylonian Empire had conquered southern Israel (Judah), and taken away all the political, religious, and social leader to Babylon. The Medes later conquered Babylon, and, in turn, the Persians defeated the Medes. The Persian Empire had a different way of dealing with their vanquished foes. They allowed the exiled people to return, to live and worship as they wished, as long as they served the Empire and were loyal (much like the Roman Empire would do centuries later). It may be that the religion of the Persians, Zoroastrianism, was the reason for this, for it was an open and inclusive religion.

An ancient Persian artifact, called the Cyrus Cylinder,[1] contains a decree much like the one mentioned in Ezra 1: the captives were allowed to return, they should rebuild their cities and temples, and live as they wished under an appointed governor. So this decree has reliable historical evidence.

We might wonder why a pagan ruler such as Cyrus would call the God of Israel "The LORD, the God of heaven," for we have no evidence that he was a believer. and pray that their God "be with them." This is the first time in the Bible that this phrase is used in the

---

[1] Discovered in 1879 by archaeologist Hormonz Rassam during excavations at Babylon.

Bible. It may be that Cyrus is merely referring to a universal God, and it means something different to him than it does to the Jews. It is also possible that Cyrus asked the Jewish leaders (perhaps Ezra himself) to compose the decree, which he then reviewed and signed.

For our purposes, the prayer is more interesting. Is Cyrus praying that the God of Israel be with them? But we must remember that pagans believed in many gods, and so, it would be no problem for Cyrus to ask the God of the Jews to be with the Jews.

The giving of neighbors reminds us of when God delivered the Jews from slavery in Egypt when they were allowed to take goods from their neighbors (Ex. 3:21-22; 11:2; 12:35-36). It is not surprising that the author would want to make a connection to that event: the Exodus and the Exile are two major events in all the history of Israel. Ezra often makes allusions to the Exodus: while this might have been a small event among many for the Persians, it was as momentous to the Jews as the Exodus from Egypt. Once again, God has delivered his people from captivity in a foreign land to the promised land.

Application

How might a prayer that "God be with them," offered by a pagan king, be any kind of model for our prayers? Of course, we can mimic the intent, and offer our own petitions that God be with someone or some group.

The context can provide us two other lessons about prayer. First, if a pagan king can pray that God be with His people, then surely we can pray for nonbelievers? Not just that they might come to faith, but that God be with them. It might seem strange to pray that God "be with" someone who does not worship or believe in Him, but we should remember that all people are God's children. If a human child rejected their parent, or did not know who they were, a loving parent would still love that child and want the best for them.

The prayer also gives us something to pray *about*. God's work in history, and in our lives, may often surprise us. Here, he uses a pagan King who practices Zoroastrianism as the conduit to return His people to their land. Moreover, Isaiah 44-54 describes Cyrus as a "savior" of the Jewish people, one who was anointed by God and a shepherd. The same concepts, of course, are used for the coming Messiah, Jesus, for a much more profound and more significant delivery of God's people. Our prayers for God's work can take into account God's surprising work throughout history and in our own lives, which leads us to praise and thank him for his grace and steadfast love.

Patience in Prayer and the Joy of God's Answers (Ezra 3.11)

> *...they sang responsively, praising and giving thanks to the LORD,*
> *"For he is good,*
> *for his steadfast love endures forever toward Israel."*

This prayer is an oft-cited prayer, found many times throughout the Bible, especially in the Psalms. Here, the context teaches us about patience in prayer and the joy of God's answers.

Background

After King Cyrus of Persia proclaimed that the Jewish exiles could return to their land and rebuild their temple, preparations were made, and the people left. Ezra describes the number and tribes of people who went back: twelve leaders, lay families, priests, Levites, and other temple officials—almost 50,000 people![1]

After they had made the trek, and settled into towns around Jerusalem, the High Priest Jeshua, other priests,

---

[1] The list may be the total amount who returned over a period of time, not all who went in the first trip.

and the governor Zerubbabel built a new altar upon the foundation of the old one and began offering sacrifices morning and celebrated the Feast of Tabernacles (or Booths). They began to practice all the daily, weekly, seasonal, and yearly worship, celebrations, and sacrifices.

During the second year, they began to work on rebuilding the Temple. Once the foundation was finished, the priest the priests and Levites celebrated with trumpets and cymbals, singing responsive songs and praising God with the prayer above.

Meaning

The description of the people who returned and the place and work of the sacrifices show that the people are returning to the same place and same practices as before—a sign of faithfulness. The description of the rebuilding of the Temple is worded to remind the readers of the original building of the first Temple, emphasizing the continuity with the past.[2]

The prayer that they sang, found so often in the Psalms, is a praise and thanksgiving to God's enduring faithfulness.[3] It celebrates the fact that God is the definition of faithfulness, because his promises last forever,

---

[2] Compare verse 7 to 1 Chron 22:2-4; 2 Chron 2:15-16; the date verse 8 to 2 Chron 3:2; the time of rebuilding (two plus five years) in 6:15 with 1 Kings 6:38; the role of the Levites in supervision (8-9) with 1 Chron 23:4.

[3] See Pslms 100:4–5; 106:1; 107:1; 118:1; 136:1.

and he loves forever. These people, eighty years later, see that God kept his promise to return them to the land.

Many of the people who were taken into exile to Babylon knew of God's promise to restore them, but died before it came to fruition. We can suppose that some of them gave up on Him, and perhaps turned to the Babylonian gods, who seems more powerful at the time. But those who did not would remember two things to help them: the constant phrase found in the Bible "wait on the Lord" and the prayer above "for his steadfast love endures forever." God's timing is not our timing—we are an impatient people!

Application

This prayer and its circumstances give us an opportunity to consider own patience in waiting for God, faithfulness during long, difficult stretches of time, and the joy that comes in restoration.

Think of a time (perhaps now) when you are waiting for something, and God seems to be offering no direction or answer. Can you still pray the prayer above? Even if it seems insincere because of your impatience (and perhaps even irritation) with God, you could pray for patience: "God, I believe, help me in my unbelief!"

Finally, can you think of a time or an event where restoration, or healing, or reconciliation came to you? Even if it was long ago, you are now living the fruits of God's restoration, and you can offer the same praise that the Jews offered above.

Take some time today to consider these issues: waiting for God, faithfulness in difficult times, and joy of restoration. What prayers can you offer today in light of them?

Living Faithfully Under a Non-Believing State (Ezra 6.12)

May the God who has established his name there overthrow any king or people that shall put forth a hand to alter this, or to destroy this house of God in Jerusalem.

Just as God used King Cyrus of Persia to further his plans for the Jews, and Cyrus offered a prayer to him, King Darius of Persia did the same, many years later. What do these prayers by unbelievers teach us about prayer and the work of God? How should a believer live under a State that does not share that faith?

Background

After the last prayer, the Jews begin rebuilding the Temple. Not without problems, though: twice they had to stop because of opposition from people who were still living in the land. These were probably descendants of people whom Assyrian had moved into the land, perhaps also intermarried with the Israelites who had never been taken into Exile. They wanted to help build the Temple, but the Returnees refused. This might seem harsh, but it was based on Israel's history. They remembered how Joshua had allowed people to stay in the promised land, and their pagan-influenced culture caused problems until the Exile. They would not make the same mistake again.

The people of the land took action against them, and caused the reconstruction to stop. But years later, they began again, and a local governor write to King Darius, the current king of the Persians, asking him if they had the authority to do so. He searched the archives and found King Cyrus' order that they rebuild the Temple. Darius sent a letter back, saying that they had authority. He went further—the governor was to help them with anything they needed, out of the royal funds, just as Cyrus had decreed. Darius closes the letter with the prayer above.

Meaning

Like with the proclamation of King Cyrus in chapter 1, this declaration of King Darius, and its prayer, may surprise us. Why is pagan king helping the Jews with their Temple, and even offering a prayer for them to their God? Of course, part of the answer is that God was using these rulers to further his own purposes for his people.

But there is a non-theological reason, too. Discoveries of ancient Persian administrative records show that the Persians believed in supporting the religions of the different peoples they ruled over. Unlike the Assyrians and Babylonians, who destroyed temples and forced people to worship Babylonians gods, the Persians believed that diversity of religion was a better way to rule.

Living Faithfully Under a Non-Believing State (Ezra 6.12)

Being polytheists, they had no trouble believing that the God of Israel was a real god, even if they did not believe he was the only god, or that they did not worship him. Therefore, the proclamation and prayer by Darius are not surprising when we understand the historical context.

Beyond that, ancient people believed that gods were localized: the Persian gods lived in Persian, the Egyptian gods in Egypt, and so on. That is where they had power. They might be able to extend it beyond their regions, at times, but mostly they worked in their own lands. So it would be natural for them to think that the God of the Jews ruled Palestine, and therefore it was smart to ask him to ensure peace in the land as the Jews rebuilt.

But the writers of the Bible are more interested in God's work, and it is clear that God is the one who caused the Persians to have this attitude, so he could then use it for his purposes in history (see 5:1–5 and 6:14, 22).

The prayer itself is a simple petition. It begins by noting that God is the God of that region, then asking him to stop anyone to tries to prevent the work of the Jews.

What can we learn from this prayer? After all, the modern world is almost the opposite of that world in many ways. Polytheism is rare, and the three major religions of the modern world all trace their origins back to the same God—the God of the Jews. Atheism did not exist in that world; it is common in ours. Finally, at least in the United States, there is an intentional separation between the State and the Church.

Still, the Persian state was no worshipper of God—but he used them for his purposes. It is no different than today, whether a government is a theocracy, agnostic, secular, or hostile to religion. God can still use them.

The Bible seems to suggest there is room for both government and the church. Their work might overlap in some areas, but their spheres of influence are (or should be) different. Their driving force is (or should be) different. The church should not be a business, or a special interest group, or a social justice movement (though it might do some similar things.) It is the body of Christ, as his ambassador on earth, to serve others, teach the Gospel, and bring others to salvation and into the church.

Application

While State leaders might not pray to our God on our behalf, we can certainly pray for them, and allow them authority in our lives (where it does not clash with God's authority). Daniel 4.17 indicates that God is the one who places people in power, believers or not. Jesus and writers of the New Testament letters say the same (Matt 22:15–22; Rom 13:1–7; 1 Pet 2:13–17).

The difficulty comes when a State forces its citizens to do something that is in direct conflict with God's commands. When that happens, believers are not to become political revolutionaries to overthrow, but merely to passively resist: as Jesus did, as the early Apostles

Living Faithfully Under a Non-Believing State (Ezra 6.12)

did in Jerusalem, and as the writer of Revelation urges his readers. (See also 1 Peter 2.)

Think today of how your local, state, national government both helps and hurts the practice of your faith. Pray for the leaders, that God will use them as he sees fit, and that you will know how to live faithfully under that State.

Praying for Secular Leaders and Government (Ezra 7.27-28)

Blessed be the LORD, the God of our ancestors, who put such a thing as this into the heart of the king to glorify the house of the LORD in Jerusalem, and who extended to me steadfast love before the king and his counselors, and before all the king's mighty officers. I took courage, for the hand of the LORD my God was upon me, and I gathered leaders from Israel to go up with me.

The separation of Church and State is written into the U.S. Constitution, a result of modern historical realities. But for believers, the separation—and connections—is found even in the ancient book of Ezra. This prayer gives us some insights into how prayer plays a part in the interaction between the State and our faith.

Background

Following the completion of the Temple, the Jews celebrated the festival of Passover. This first section of the book of Ezra ends there, and the rest of the book is about (or by) Ezra himself. The time between chapter 6 and chapter 7 is almost 60 years.

Ezra was a priest and a descendant of the high priest before the Exile. But he was also a scribe—the people who became more important when there was no Temple, because their focus was on scripture. Ezra is often presented in the Bible as a "second Moses" because of his leading, teaching, and holding the people accountable to God's ways.

He travels to Jerusalem, commissioned by King Artaxerxes I, to accomplish four things. First, he was to take a group to Jerusalem from Babylon. Second, he was to deliver gifts and money to the Temple and ensure that proper funds flowed to the Temple in the future. Third, he was to make sure that the Temple and the practices were being done properlyaccording to the Jewish law. The final task was to teach the people who lived outside of Jerusalem how to live under the Jewish laws.

All of this was written in a document and signed by the King. Immediately following the words of the King's declaration, Ezra offers the prayer above, as a response of blessing upon God for His provision of the Temple and their return to worship and live under Him.

Meaning

The third part of the King's decree might surprise some, but, as we have noted before, the Persians encouraged the religion of their conquered people. This might be what lies behind the issue of mixed-religion marriages later in the book, for such marriages could bring prob-

Praying for Secular Leaders and Government (Ezra 7.27-28)

lems for living under the Jewish law if one spouse was not Jewish.

Ezra's reaction to the document put forth by the king is to offer a prayer of blessing upon God. While the document is an important one for the history of Persia and especially for the Jewish people, Ezra's focus is that God has kept his promise by expressing his long-suffering love to his people. Further, it is that the center of worship for God's people, the Temple, is being provided for and protected. A lot has happened since God called Abram to be the beginning of a nation under God, but he is still the same God, the "the God of our fathers" (v27), who uses a pagan king to continue his promises.

The prayer itself is a blessing-prayer (or a benediction). It is a simple prayer, and resembles many of the prayers of praise found in the Psalms. Like we have seen so often, this blessing on God is a direct response to what God has done for the Jews.

The prayer shows that Ezra is honored and humbled to be called to be part of God's plan. Yet it also shows that he is aware that this is a historical change—the relationship between State and the religion of the Jews has changed. In the past, the government was either a theocracy, under God, or under a foreign power who was hostile to God. In Ezra's time, the two are different but work together. This will eventually lead to the message found in the New Testament that all people can be citizens of God's kingdom, regardless of their citizenship in this world, while at the same time living under a

State's authority and even praying for the secular leaders.

Application

Strikingly, this new partnership between the State and religion in ancient times is not that different from many Western democracies today. The State and the Church are not the same and have different goals, yet the State encourages faith communities. At the same time, a State's policies can sometimes work against it. As noted in previous studies, God's people are called to be submissive to the State, which God uses, but also to remember that they are first part of God's kingdom. What the State does is of little concern.

Do you pray for your secular and governmental leaders? Ezra, Jesus, and the New Testament writers believe you should. Even when you disagree with their policies or philosophy of government, you can pray for their safety and wisdom, for God can use them to further His purposes just as He used King Artaxerxes I.

Prayer and Fasting Go Together (Ezra 8.21)

Then I proclaimed a fast there, at the river Ahava, that we might deny ourselves before our God, to seek from him a safe journey for ourselves, our children, and all our possessions.
So we fasted and petitioned our God for this, and he listened to our entreaty.

Do you fast as a spiritual exercise? For ancient Jews and Christians, fasting was almost exclusively used in conjunction with prayer—petition, to be precise. This story of Ezra, fasting, and prayer demonstrate why fasting and prayer go together.

Background

The author of Ezra then lists all the people who returned to Judah from Babylon with Ezra (8.1-14). The total number was probably more than 5,000 men, women, and children. They gathered and camped for three days by a canal that ran into Babylon. Ezra took stock of the people and realized that there were no Levites among them. He sent messengers back to Babylon and found some Levite families willing to join the group.

Ezra then ordered everyone to partake in fasting and praying to God, to ask for a safe journey and protection along the way back to Jerusalem. Only then did they set out. Once there, they offered sacrifices to God for keeping them safe.

Meaning

There are three themes emphasized in this passage. While all three suggest that Ezra was fulfilling King Artaxerxes' edict, they also demonstrate that he was only able to do so with God's help.

The first one is when Ezra discovers that they have no Levites among their group. They are the ones who were supposed to carry the religious vessels according to the law of Moses. When Ezra sent the word out, the quick and numerous response was God's doing, even though it also fulfilled the edict by taking care of their religious duties as the king had commanded.

The second theme comes from Ezra's refusal to ask the king for an armed escort—he believed God would protect them if they relied on Him (which He did). Related to this is the third theme, that the caravan was carrying so much wealth that it would be especially attractive to attack.

It might seem that Ezra and the people were relying on "spiritual" protection and ignored—even refusing—to take any physical precautions. But this is incorrect. Having the Levites with them, who knew how to care for and protect the vessels, was at Ezra's command. In

Prayer and Fasting Go Together (Ezra 8.21)

fact, many precautions were taken to guard them (see vv25-30 and 33-34).

We might say, "Yes, but Ezra refused a Persian guard, relying only on God." Yet that is not what happened. Ezra had repeatedly told the king how powerful God was, and that He protected his people and was quick to defend them with his wrath. Ezra was embarrassed to ask the king for a guard (v22), because it might seem that he didn't trust God after all.

Any separation of the "spiritual" and the "physical" comes from Greek philosophy, not the Bible. God is part of both, and they are intimately intertwined. To separate them is to separate what God has created to be one.

There is an old story that exemplifies this erroneous concept.

> *A man was trapped on his rooftop in a flood. He prayed to God for help. Soon, a man in a rowboat came by, and man inside shouted to the man on the roof, "Jump in, I can save you." The stranded fellow shouted back, "No, it's okay, I'm praying to God, and he is going to save me." So the rowboat went on.*
>
> *Then a motorboat came by. The fellow in the motorboat shouted up, "Jump in; I can save you." But the stranded man said, "No, thanks, I'm praying to God, and he is going to save me. I have faith." So the motorboat went on.*
>
> *Then a helicopter came by, and the pilot shouted down, "Grab this rope, and I'll lift you*

to safety." The stranded man again replied, "No thanks, I'm praying to God, and he is going to save me. I have faith." So the helicopter flew away.

Soon the water rose, and the man drowned. He went to Heaven and appeared before God. He exclaimed, "I had faith in you, but you didn't save me, you let me drown. Why?!"

God replied, "I sent you a rowboat, a motorboat, and a helicopter. What more did you want?"

God almost always works through people and the physical things he has created. After all, it all belongs to him. This leads us to fasting, for it makes a connection between the physical (our need for food and drink) and the spiritual (talking with God).

When the people with Ezra fasted and prayed, the text says that they "humbled" themselves. The Hebrew word used here is different than the one used in similar contexts in Chronicles—here it is almost the word "afflicting," meaning that they are asking God to care for them and protect them because they cannot do it themselves.

Fasting is rarely mentioned in writings from the ancient world, only perhaps during mourning. In the Bible, fasting is often connected with asking God for something, as in this passage. The practice became more widely practiced during this period after the Exile.[1] The idea behind fasting is to focus on the spiri-

---

[1] See Ezra 10:6; Neh 9:1; Esth 4:3, 16; Isa 58:3; Joel 1–2.

tual need, to remind ourselves that we are dependent on God for survival (food), and thus it is a way to humble ourselves.

Application

There are two things we can focus on from this passage about prayer. First, that we should not, as believers, allows a disconnect between the physical and the spiritual. They are one, created by God.

Fasting is an excellent way to remind us of this as we pray. Trying fasting for a meal, and instead of eating, pray and read scripture. You might try two meals or even 24 hours. As the hunger pangs set in, you can recall how God has created us to need sustenance, and then how he has provided food through plants and animals. As you get thirsty, remember that he made us that way, and then provided sources of water and other liquids. He sustains us daily, and we are entirely dependent on him.

That physical dependence on Him reminds us that we are also dependent on him in many others ways: for a purpose in life, for the blessings we have, and for our salvation.

Fasting reminds us of our dependence on his incredible grace, and on his protection, as we come before him, with humility, to offer our petitions.

Prayer and Divorce? (Ezra 10.1-11)

While Ezra prayed and made confession, weeping and throwing himself down before the house of God, a very great assembly of men, women, and children gathered to him out of Israel; the people also wept bitterly.

Now make confession to the LORD the God of your ancestors, and do his will; separate yourselves from the peoples of the land and from the foreign wives."

Why, in this story, is divorce the solution to the people's sin? There are other passages of scripture which declare that God hates divorce. It is the context of the story that can help us understand the prayer, the divorce, and the terrible and unintended consequences of wrongdoing.

Background

These two prayers are part of the same series of events as the last prayer (9.6-15). Ezra had been told that many of the men had married women who were not of the Jewish faith—women whose people had been living in the land for centuries, not part of the returnees from exile. Ezra confesses to God his failure.

While he prays, a large group of Jews come to him, weeping (and presumably praying) with him. One of the leaders suggests to Ezra, that they all make a new covenant with God and that they divorce these wives. He insists it be done properly under the Jewish law. Ezra instructed the priests to follow this plan, and give the people three days to assemble and comply. He then went to the newly-rebuilt Temple. He spent the night there, fasting and in mourning.

After three days, the people gathered in the square before the Temple. Ezra told them that they had been faithless to God by marrying foreign women, so they must confess, repent, and then work to be a separate people. The people affirmed that they had sinned, and that they would do as he said, but asked for a long-term plan because it would be a significant undertaking.

Meaning

Most readers would read this story and be confused, and focus more on the solution (divorce) than the prayer itself. After all are many other passages in the Bible which declare that divorce was never a part of God's plan for humans.

To understand the prayer, we have first to understand the situation. In the creation story, when God creates a woman, the two "become one" and the implication is that they will not separate (Gen 2.18-24). In the Law of Moses, the command is given that, in many cases, divorce is not permitted (Deut 22.19, 29). However, in

Prayer and Divorce? (Ezra 10.1-11)

some cases, divorce was allowed (Deut 24; Isa 50.1; Jer 3.8), and this became a subject of debate among the rabbis—what was required for a divorce to be allowed under the law? Jesus entered into the debate with these words:

> *"It was also said, 'Whoever divorces his wife, let him give her a certificate of divorce.' But I say to you that anyone who divorces his wife, except on the ground of unchastity, causes her to commit adultery; and whoever marries a divorced woman commits adultery. (Matt 5.31ff)*

He takes an even stronger stand later when questioned about it:

> *Some Pharisees came to him, and to test him they asked, "Is it lawful for a man to divorce his wife for any cause?" He answered, "Have you not read that the one who made them at the beginning 'made them male and female,' and said, 'For this reason a man shall leave his father and mother and be joined to his wife, and the two shall become one flesh'? So they are no longer two, but one flesh. Therefore what God has joined together, let no one separate." They said to him, "Why then did Moses command us to give a certificate of dismissal and to divorce her?" He said to them, "It was because you were so hard-hearted that Moses allowed you to divorce your wives, but from the beginning it was not so. And I say to you, whoever divorces*

his wife, except for unchastity, and marries another commits adultery." (Matt 19.3-9; see also Mark 10)

The Pharisees and others want to know the answer to the question, "when can I get a divorce?" But Jesus says that it is the wrong question! Instead, he focuses on the meaning of marriage—it is meant to be a covenant that is never to be broken, just like God never breaks his promises. But, Jesus concedes, humans are weak, and we sometimes treat others so terribly that they must leave (consider spousal abuse, for example). Paul echoes these teachings in 1 Corinthians 7—even when one is a nonbeliever, which is in direct contrast to the story of Ezra! (See also 1 Peter 3.1-7).

What do we make of this? The key lies in understanding that those that came from Exile back to Jerusalem were in a precarious and unusual situation. To survive in a land filled with pagans, having come from a land of pagans, they needed a strong sense of their own identity as Jewish people. To have wives and in-laws who worship other gods would create a situation where there would be pressure (stated or unstated) to compromise their faith.

That principle is no less true today, but our situation is rarely (if ever) the same. Certainly marriage to a nonbeliever might affect a believer negatively. But it will not affect the faith of the entire people of God! Yet for those people, and Ezra, it did. It was not unlike when God first sent the Hebrews into the promised land, which was filled with people who worshipped other Gods. Back then, for the same reasons, he told them not to intermarry. (Ex 34:11–16; Deut 7:1–5).

Some have taken this passage, and the words of Jesus, to mean that if a believer marries an unbeliever, they should divorce. Of course, the words of Paul speak against this. Instead, we should see this as an example of how God understands our weaknesses. There are rules about the best way to live, but God is not a legalist. He commands us not to divorce not to punish us when we do, but to remind us of the importance of marriage! Once we fail, the law matters not—now that it's done, what will we do? In the case of Ezra, the stakes were high and divorce was the only answer. (We should note here, too that sin often leads to bad consequences.)

Application

We will not find ourselves in a situation where our decisions about marriage (or anything else) will affect the entire people of God, and put them in danger of apostasy. But we can learn from their example. When Ezra confronted the people, they were honest about their failure: "It is so; we must do as you have said" (10.13). We can do the same: when we recognize our sin, we admit it and confess.

The other element that can enrich our prayers is the effect we see of sin. Not only does sin have consequences for us, and probably for others, but also the solution to the situation created by sin the might be bad. The Jews in this story, not remembering why they were there, sinned by marrying unbelievers. The only solution, to save the community, was divorces—a bad solution with terrible human consequences.

Offer honest prayers of confession when required. And remember that sin can have consequences far beyond the immediate—we can pray for strength to make right decisions, too.

Pure Confession—no requests, no excuses, no reasons (Ezra 9.6-15)

"O my God, I am too ashamed and embarrassed to lift my face to you, my God, for our iniquities have risen higher than our heads, and our guilt has mounted up to the heavens. From the days of our ancestors to this day we have been deep in guilt, and for our iniquities we, our kings, and our priests have been handed over to the kings of the lands, to the sword, to captivity, to plundering, and to utter shame, as is now the case. But now for a brief moment favor has been shown by the LORD our God, who has left us a remnant, and given us a stake in his holy place, in order that he may brighten our eyes and grant us a little sustenance in our slavery. For we are slaves; yet our God has not forsaken us in our slavery, but has extended to us his steadfast love before the kings of Persia, to give us new life to set up the house of our God, to repair its ruins, and to give us a wall in Judea and Jerusalem.

"And now, our God, what shall we say after this? For we have forsaken your commandments, which you commanded by your servants the prophets, saying, 'The land that you are

entering to possess is a land unclean with the pollutions of the peoples of the lands, with their abominations. They have filled it from end to end with their uncleanness. Therefore do not give your daughters to their sons, neither take their daughters for your sons, and never seek their peace or prosperity, so that you may be strong and eat the good of the land and leave it for an inheritance to your children forever.' After all that has come upon us for our evil deeds and for our great guilt, seeing that you, our God, have punished us less than our iniquities deserved and have given us such a remnant as this, shall we break your commandments again and intermarry with the peoples who practice these abominations? Would you not be angry with us until you destroy us without remnant or survivor? O LORD, God of Israel, you are just, but we have escaped as a remnant, as is now the case. Here we are before you in our guilt, though no one can face you because of this."

What is a prayer of confession? Often, such prayers are an admittance of guilt followed by a petition for forgiveness. But this prayer, by Ezra, is a pure prayer of confession—no requests, no excuses, no reasons. A difficult prayer to offer, but one of power.

Pure Confession—no requests, no excuses, no reasons (Ezra 9.6-15)

Background

The rest of the book of Ezra describes the reforms that Ezra instituted. There are three prayers in the section: the first is this one, a prayer of confession offered by Ezra himself. They are all part of the same situation.

What brought on this confession? About fourth months had passed, it seems, since the last scene (see 10.3). Part of what Ezra was to do in Jerusalem was to teach the proper ways of faith. Some officials came to him and said that there was a problem with the people having married non-believers—even leaders and religious officials.

Ezra, upon hearing this, tore his cloak and pulled out his hair and beard, in a traditional sign of mourning and repentance. He fasted—another humbling tradition—until the evening sacrifice. He then prayed the prayer above, confessing his embarrassment at the situation. He does not ask for anything; he merely confesses the sin of his people and himself.

He begins with his own shame and also prays on behalf of the people (vv6-7). He noes how merciful God has been for them in the past, which makes this unfaithfulness all the more terrible (vv8-9). He cites the sin specifically in vv10-11:

> *And now, our God, what shall we say after this? For we have forsaken your commandments, 11 which you commanded by your servants the prophets, saying, 'The land that you are entering to possess is a land unclean with*

75

the pollutions of the peoples of the lands, with their abominations. They have filled it from end to end with their uncleanness.

Finally, he notes that God would be justified in destroying all of them since they have spat in the face of His mercies.

Meaning

Why this great humility and guilt over marrying unbelievers? There are a number of factors at play. First, Ezra and the returnees to Jerusalem were tasked with restoring the faith and practice of Israel, in all its commands. Second, Ezra was responsible, for it is he that the king of Persia had commissioned to rebuild the Temple and restore the faithful life of the community of returnees. Third, the people are in a different situation now than back in Babylon, where they were a community surrounded by Persians. Here, they were surrounded by people who were descendants of the Jews who were left behind, but who had intermarried with pagans over the 80+ years of the Exile. They were facing a cultural shift and only just realizing the problems it could bring.

They reasoned this way: when God brought the Israelites out of Egypt and into the Promised Land, he forbid them to intermarry with the Canaanites. Why? Because God knew that they would be affected by their worship practices, and that it would cause them to stray

Pure Confession—no requests, no excuses, no reasons (Ezra 9.6-15)

from God's ways.[1] Joshua was even ordered to destroy all the towns and people for this reason. But he did not, and decades later we see that the people did stray because of the influence of the Canaanites who remaining in the land.

Ezra and the others applied these teachings, and the history to their situation—those who had married unbelievers were sure to bring problems to this new generation. A spouse or a child would be put in a difficult position of mixing faith traditions.

So Ezra believed he had failed God in not foreseeing this problem and addressing it early on. Now, the cost to lives and families would be painful. This is why his prayer is purely a prayer of confession. He acknowledges that God would be justified in destroying them all, because now, no matter what they do, people will suffer.

This is why Ezra adopts the traditions of mourning for the dead—because if God meted out justice, they would all die.

Application

A prayer of pure confession is a powerful thing. We are tempted, when we confess our wrongdoing, to give reasons why it happened; to ask for forgiveness; to even blame others, perhaps!

---

[1] See Lev 18; 19:19; Deut 7:1-4, 20:10-18.

Try offering a prayer of pure confession. Don't ask for forgiveness, don't give reasons why you did it, and don't repent. Just tell God what you did, and praise Him for who He is and how he is justified to punish. Such a prayer brings into stark relief how meaningful it is when God offers his grace to us.

It is not an easy thing to do! But it is a powerful and rich prayer that speaks truth to the situation between God and his people.

Summary of the Prayers of Ezra

The prayers found in the book of Ezra take place during a unique time in the history of Israel: the King of Persia sends Ezra to lead a large group of Jews back to their homeland after decades of exile. They are to rebuild the Temple and restore their religious practices and worship.

In such a unique period, we might think the prayer would be so specific that they would offer us little to learn for our own prayers. But, like so many other prayers in the Bible, there are always new perspective and insights.

The surprise that a pagan king would offer prayers to God for believers tells us that God can act in ways that we might never expect (Ezra 1.3). Our prayers can be bold, out-of-the-box kinds of requests. It also tells us that God is concerned about the history of both believers and unbelievers, and we can pray for our own political and community leaders.

We also learn how to pray a prayer of praise and thanks when God answers our prayers. Sometimes we are better at asking for things than thanking Him for what he has given us—and the prayer in 3.11 is a good reminder.

The last four prayers in Ezra (and in fact, the rest of the book from chapter 6 on) have a lot to teach us about how to live faithfully when surrounded by an unbelieving culture. We can pray for our leaders (both church and political), and we can ask for guidance when our nation encourages or forces us to do things we believe are against the will of God (6.12; 7.27-28). In the midst of these last prayers, we find a prayer about fasting and how we can connect it to our prayer life (8.21).

In the last two prayers, we get to focus on prayers of confession—a type of prayer that we may not practice too often—especially not public confession, perhaps even rarer in today's world (9.6-15; 10.1-11). Prayers of confession should be honest, leaving all excuses or reasons aside. We could even leave out asking for forgiveness—just confess! (Asking for mercy could come in a later prayer).

The last lesson we learn from these prayers is that, since our wrongdoing can have consequences beyond just ourselves and those we sinned against, we should pray both for those affected, and that we will babe the strength to avoid hurting others in the future.

Introduction to the Prayers in Nehemiah

As the book of Ezra focused on rebuilding the Temple and learning to be faithful, so the book of Nehemiah focuses on rebuilding the walls of the city and learning to be faithful. These themes are also found in the prayers, and provide an excellent study for our own prayers when we seek renewal of our faith.

The person of Nehemiah, along with Ezra, are two of the greatest men in Israelite history. They were key figures in bringing the Jews back from Exile and creating a new community after the destruction of the Temple.

There are 17 prayer passages in the book of Nehemiah.

Contents

The books of Ezra and Nehemiah were one book but were separated into two during the third century AD by the theologians Origen and Jerome.

There is some debate about the dates of Ezra and Nehemiah's work, though most think Nehemiah came to work under Artaxerxes I.

One interesting and unusual aspect of Nehemiah is the passages that are in first person—Nehemiah himself speaking to us. Some of the passages are his verbatim prayers.

Nehemiah was the cupbearer to Artaxerxes I of Persia. He received a report that the exiles in Jerusalem were having difficulties and that the wall protecting the city was in bad repair. He asked the king if he could go to rebuild the city and its walls. The king agreed, and sent him along with letters to the officials there, describing his task and permission to use timber from the forests.

Once there, he began working to rebuild the wall and rebuff many of the surrounding enemies who had been troubling the people.

Nehemiah then encouraged more people to come to the city. He also helped Ezra with purifying the faith and insisting the Temple and the people remain faithful to the practices and laws of the Jews.

He was governor for twelve years, then returned to the king services for a time. When he went back to Jerusalem, he found they had fallen back into their old ways, and he once again purified the temple and the priesthood, reinforcing observance of the laws.

Themes

The book of Nehemiah focuses more on the political and social problems than Ezra, but the theological dimensions are connected, of course.

"Remembrance" is a major theme, and found in four of the prayers (5.19; 13.14, 22, 31). The request is for God to remember all Nehemiah has done, but this theme also flows into passages and prayers, where the people are to remember what God has done for them (both in the past and present).

A follower of God is to have a certain "identity:" people should be able to tell a difference between people who follow God and those who do not. Since much of Nehemiah is concerned with faithfulness and living properly before God, much of it (and its prayers) stress the characteristics that God's people should have. They (and we) are God's people, who he has saved and redeemed. Therefore, we should live like it.

Connected to the theme of identity is the theme of loyalty to God. The book notes the many times the Israelites have been unfaithful to God, despite all of his love and care (and punishments). The book and its prayers offer a call to remain loyal in all circumstances.

Confidence is also a strong theme of the book. Both Ezra and Nehemiah believedÂ fully in God and what he called them to do, and they do not give up. Rebuilding the wall was difficult—constant attacks from outsiders and insiders were frequent. Yet Nehemiah never gave up, urging the people on in the name of God.Â

The last important theme is one that many of us in the modern world don't like: rules for living. Modern western culture prefers a more free and open approach to life, with each individual deciding for themselves—no one should tell us what to do! But the message of Nehemiah is that God can tell us what to do—not only because he created us, but because he knows the best way for us to live.

The Prayers

There are 17 prayers in Nehemiah, ranging from mere mentions of prayer to a lengthy section of praises, thanksgivings, and petitions in chapter 9. That prayer (offered by priests, singers, and a long one by Nehemiah) exemplifies all the prayers found in the book.

The focus of the book is rebuilding, protecting, and renewing the people of God. As such, it focuses on confession and repentance for past unfaithfulness, petitions for God to protect them and lead them, vows and curses to hold all accountable, and praises and thanksgivings for the second chance that God has given the people of Israel.

The prayers then stand as excellent examples of prayers when we seek forgiveness, spiritual renewal, and help from God for us to be faithful and devoted.Â

Calling and Prayer (Neh 1.5-11)

I said, "O LORD God of heaven, the great and awesome God who keeps covenant and steadfast love with those who love him and keep his commandments; 6 let your ear be attentive and your eyes open to hear the prayer of your servant that I now pray before you day and night for your servants, the people of Israel, confessing the sins of the people of Israel, which we have sinned against you. Both my family and I have sinned. 7 We have offended you deeply, failing to keep the commandments, the statutes, and the ordinances that you commanded your servant Moses. 8 Remember the word that you commanded your servant Moses, 'If you are unfaithful, I will scatter you among the peoples; 9 but if you return to me and keep my commandments and do them, though your outcasts are under the farthest skies, I will gather them from there and bring them to the place at which I have chosen to establish my name.' 10 They are your servants and your people, whom you redeemed by your great power and your strong hand. 11 O Lord, let your ear be attentive to the prayer of your servant, and to the prayer of your servants who delight in revering

*your name. Give success to your servant today,
and grant him mercy in the sight of this man!"*

Sometimes God calls us to do unexpected things—perhaps life-changing, perhaps just altering a daily course. But rather than dive right into action, the right thing might be to spend time in serious, open prayer, like Nehemiah.

Background

The book begins as a first-person narrative by Nehemiah, who is a cup-bearer to the king—that is, he brought wine to the king. But it meant more than that. He would have often been close to the king and his harem, and were often eunuchs, though there is no indication that Nehemiah was one. He may have served as the king's wine-taster, bearer of the signet ring, and his financial advisor. As such, he would have had direct access to the king, which will play an important role later when he approaches the king with his wishes to help his people.

One day, in discussion with another Jew, Nehemiah learns that those who had returned to Jerusalem were in trouble because the walls of the city are in disrepair and the gates had been destroyed. This news affected Nehemiah profoundly. He cried, mourned, fasted, and prayed for days. He recorded the words (or some of the words) of his prayer.

After asking God to hear him, he confesses the sins of himself, his family, and all of Israel. He then reminds God that, while punishment had come to them as they

Calling and Prayer (Neh 1.5-11)

had been warned, God has also promised to restore them if they returned to him. Since they have done so, he asks God to hear him and give him mercy.

Meaning

The events in Jerusalem that Nehemiah hears of are probably the same events described in Ezra 4:7-23. More importantly for our purposes, however, is that Nehemiah hears this news as a calling from God. His experience and position as king's servant would have prepared him for this role. Verses 4–7 show how much he identifies with his people. Later, in 2.1, we find he has been praying about the situation for four months. This is no passing concern—he believes that God may be calling him.

The prayer switches back and forth between first person singular and plural, which may seem strange, but may be the result of either later editing, or simply Nehemiah's way of identifying with his people.

Unlike many we have studied in this project, this prayer is a combination of three prayer types. It begins with a praise which leads to a first petition that God hear him. Then, he offers a prayer of confession and repentance, both personally and for the entire people of Israel (6-7). A second petition comes next (8-11). Using God's own promises to his people, he asks him that he would both restore the people, and help him approach the king properly.

Some have suggested that this is a lament prayer, but it does not contain the despair and questions of "why?" that laments do. Nehemiah *knows* why—the people had sinned against God, which is why he includes a prayer of confession.

Application

There are a couple of ways we might use this prayer as a model for our own prayers.

Structure. Follow the structure of this prayer, but add your own content:

1. An address to God (v5)

2. Ask for God to hear your prayer (v6a)

3. Confess your sins (vv6b-7)

4. Appeal to God's promises (vv8-10

5. Petitions and intercessions (v11)

Calling. Have you ever felt that God was calling you to do something? Did prayer play a role? Notice how Nehemiah, who seemingly had no sense that he would ever leave the role of the King's cupbearer, felt called. But he did not just run off—he spent time in serious, focused prayer. Perhaps you don't think you have been called by God—but don't assume a "calling" is some big, career-changing event. It might just be something you need to do different, someone you need to help, some minor, but important, change. Pray about it like

Calling and Prayer (Neh 1.5-11)

Nehemiah, being patient and asking God to guide you and help you to make timely and well-thought-out actions.

Prayer and Our Responsibility to Act (Neh 2.4)

Then the king said to me, "What do you request?" So I prayed to the God of heaven.

What is the connection between prayer and action? Between God's actions and our responsibility? This story of Nehemiah and his prayers gives us the answers to those questions.

Background

Nehemiah was struggling with the news of his people in Jerusalem and had been praying about it for a month. One day, when he appeared before the King and Queen during his duties, the King noted that he seemed sad, and asked him what was wrong. Nehemiah told him of the troubles that his people were experiencing in Jerusalem. When the king asked him what he would like to do, Nehemiah prayed to God and then told the king that he would like to go and help his people rebuild the wall.

The king granted him leave to go. Emboldened, Nehemiah asked him also for letters of passage, and letters to obtain wood from the king's forest, he did that as well.

Meaning

When the king asked what was wrong, Nehemiah did not ask him to help him, he merely told him what made him so sad. Was this a sign of his trust in God? That he would not ask right now, because he was not sure what God wanted him to do? So he simply told the king the facts.

When the king asked what he wanted, Nehemiah prayed to God, as he had been for weeks. Notice the connection between this mention of prayer and the prayers he had already been offering: "the God of Heaven" (1.4, 5). He'd been preparing for this moment for a month.

Once Nehemiah knew that God had given him an opening, he became bold, and not only asked if he could go to Jerusalem to help, but also made further requests from the king to help him achieve his goal of rebuilding the wall. He had apparently been thinking about what he would ask for, should God open the door with the king.

Important for our purposes here is how Nehemiah prepared. A need of God's people was brought before him, and he wanted to act. But what did God require of him, of anything? So he prayed about it, asking God to open doors. He also *thought* about it, and what he would need to ask for if that door did open.

Yet he was also patient, waiting patiently for God to open that door. He did not force it, he did not approach the king, but merely went about his business, waiting for the opportunity. He trusts God, and so, he "waits on the Lord."

Could he have approached the king on his own initiative? Perhaps, in another situation, that might have been the proper thing to do. But in this case, Nehemiah was not even sure he was the one God wanted to accomplish the rebuilding. The wall, and the people, were in Jerusalem. He was the cupbearer to the king in Persia. So in this situation, he waited for God to show up.

Notice, however, that once God acted through the king's inquiry, Nehemiah did not hesitate. Knowing God was behind it, he pressed forward with all boldness.

Both of these elements show faithfulness in prayer: the willingness to be patient in prayer (four months), and the faith to act boldly once the path was clear.

There is also another element here that can help us in prayer. He did not *only* pray; he also planned. While he waited for God, he was doing what he could do with what he had. When God opened the door, he was ready to charge ahead with a strategy and specific needs.

Application

What can we apply to our own prayers from Nehemiah's example? First, we can reaffirm God's sovereignty. He runs his creation, and our role is to serve him through both prayer and action. Giving God his due, confessing, and asking—but also giving careful thought to our plans whole waiting for him to show us the path forward.

Second, God's actions and our responsibilities are not two separate things. If we had been in the same situation, we might have simply prayed, "God, please protect the people of Jerusalem and repair their wall." That places all the responsibility on God and none on us. We should add, "...and if there is a way that I can help, show me the opportunity and the way." This joins us with God in His work. Yet it should not end there—we should begin thinking, planning, and talking with others about how we might help out, should God give us the sign that he wants us to move ahead.

This is the practicality of prayer. It is not just words between us and God, it is not just mental intimacy. It leads to action: waiting, watching, and planning. Human responsibility, guided by the hand of God.

That is prayer as it should be.

Is It ever Appropriate to Ask God to Curse Someone? (Neh 4.4-5)

Hear, O our God, for we are despised; turn their taunt back on their own heads, and give them over as plunder in a land of captivity. Do not cover their guilt and do not let their sin be blotted out from your sight; for they have hurled insults in the face of the builders.

In this day of radical tolerance (except against those who refuse to tolerate indiscriminate tolerance), most of us are likely to judge anyone who offers a curse-prayer. Yet they are part of the Biblical tradition of prayer. What can we learn from this one, and in our age, is a curse-prayer ever appropriate?

Background

The King allowed Nehemiah to go to Jerusalem and take charge of rebuilding the wall. Once there, he met with the leaders, went out and inspected the wall. He then asked the people to join him in the task, and the response was overwhelming. They started by rebuilding the "Sheep's Gate" and worked counterclockwise around the city. Nehemiah details the work, the places on the wall rebuilt, and each group or tribe responsible for the rebuilding.

But the work is not without opposition. Nehemiah and his work anger a nearby leader, Sanballat (perhaps the governor of Syria) and Tobiah, a foreigner who lived in Jerusalem. They ridicule the wall, saying it was weak and pitiful, trying to demoralize the workers. This is happening in public, at the wall, with the workers and the tormentors face to face. Nehemiah's response is the prayer above. He asks for God not only to turn their taunts back on them, but for their land to be overrun and taken into captivity. Further, he asks that God not forgive them or forget their sin, because of their insults against God's work.

Meaning

To Nehemiah's credit, rather than fighting back with words or actions against the bullies, he turns to God in prayer. This is because he saw the criticisms and ridicule aimed more at God than himself. It only made sense that God should be the one to address the issue.

He makes it clear that God's honor is at stake, because it was God who called Nehemiah to travel to Jerusalem and help rebuild the wall. It was God who saw that the King supported him with generous amounts of money and supplies.

Nehemiah does not just pray a petition, he offers the answer—they should suffer what they are hoping others will experience. The words about their lands being

Is It ever Appropriate to Ask God to Curse Someone? (Neh 4.4-5)

plundered and captivity recall what happened to the Jews in decades and centuries past, especially King Hezekiah's prayer when he was threatened by Sennacherib (2 Kings 19.14-19).[1]

Do not "cover their guilt" refers to the blotting out of sin as part of the atonement process when one comes before God. In this case, since God himself has been impugned, their sin should not be covered.

We have discussed a number of curse-prayers since we began with the first prayer in Genesis. As we have discussed, the idea of asking God to curse someone is difficult for most of us. Perhaps the fact that these people are ridiculing God's own plan and purposes, we might understand it a bit more. Still, doesn't *everyone* at least deserve a chance to repent first and then obtain forgiveness.

Some try to soften this sort of language by saying that it's all about the context—Nehemiah believes that God himself is being insulted. Rather than taking matters into his own hands, he asks God to render punishment on them. (Would that we were more defensive of the name of God!) Moreover, we could say that imprecatory prayers (curse-prayers) were common at the time, because those people were less sophisticated than us and did not have the model and actions of Jesus to temper our prayers.

All true, of course, but what does it mean for us? We should probably be more outraged than we are when

---

[1] See also Psalms 44, 74, and 79 where similar curse prayers are offered.

people work against God's plans and ridicule Him and his people in our time. Should we pray a curse-prayer?

Application

Jesus, of course, addressed the issue of those who torment us. "Love your enemies and pray for your persecutors" (Matt 5.44, REB). Paul was even more specific, for our purposes: "Call down blessings on your persecutors—blessings, not curses" (Rom 12.14). However, these texts are about those who persecute us. What about those who attack God? In the same letter, Paul writes,

> *My dear friends, do not seek revenge, but leave a place for divine retribution; for there is a text which reads, 'Vengeance is mine, says the Lord, I will repay.' (Rom 12.19, REB)*

Paul's words apply directly to Nehemiah's prayer! But before we decide we can offer curse-prayers, read what Paul writes next:

> *But there is another text: 'If your enemy is hungry, feed him; if he is thirsty, give him a drink; by doing this you will heap live coals on his head.' (Rom 12.20, REB)*

Even more, there are passages in both the Old and New Testaments that urge God's followers to practice radical forgiveness, even when it seems ridiculous. When Peter asked Jesus how many times he should forgive some-

Is It ever Appropriate to Ask God to Curse Someone? (Neh 4.4-5)

one, Jesus told him to forgive endlessly (seventy times seven) (Matt 18.21–22). Peter reiterates that attitude and says that God's followers should have the same (1 PEt 2.20–23). It is not just the New Testament that holds these values, Paul is quoting Proverbs 25.21–22 in the passage from Roman above.[2]

But for our study of prayer, we should look to Jesus himself, as he was being tortured and killed by those who accused him falsely *as part of God's master plan*, prayed, "Father forgive them, for they don't know what they are doing."

It is clear that this is the better way—it is God's own way, Jesus' way, even in the most extreme circumstances. Does this mean that curse-prayers are no longer useful to the Christian? Perhaps we should not go that far. After all, Nehemiah did not take matters into his own hands—he turned the situation over to God. He did use a curse-prayer, but a curse-prayer asks God to act—and he can choose to ignore our request and offer grace instead.

Perhaps the best lessons from this prayer are these: like Nehemiah, we should turn retribution over to God (even if we might, at times, offer a curse-prayer); we should go beyond that often—if not always—to bless and not curse; and we should, in our prayers and actions, imitate Jesus and the rest of the Bible in offering radical forgiveness.

---

[2] See also Exod 23:4–5; Lev 19:17–18; Prov 24:17.

Does your passion match God's will? (Neh 4.9)

So we prayed to our God, and set a guard as a protection against them day and night.

When we are passionate about something, we don't want to wait around for it. We want to move ahead, make plans, take action. For a believer, there is a time to do that, rather than "waiting on the Lord." But our "passion" should not be the driving force of our actions. Prayer should play a significant part of anything we do, and Nehemiah's prayer here shows us the right way.

Background

The opposition from external and internal forces did not stop the work on the wall. The construction reached the halfway point, and this progress further enraged the opposition. Several foreign groups banded together and harass Jerusalem to cause confusion. These groups literally surrounded Jerusalem: Samballat in the north in Samaria; the "Arabs" and Edomites to the south, the Ammonites in east, and the Ashdodites lived to the west.

Rather than panic at this encircling alliance, Nehemiah's response is two-fold: he prays with his people, and then appoints a guard to a 24-hour patrol to protect the wall and the workers.

Meaning

The structure of the scene here is one we have seen, and continue to find, in Nehemiah. God's people make progress (the halfway point of the wall), but meet with opposition (the foreigners plan an attack). Nehemiah addresses the issue with prayer and then with action.

Likewise, some of the language here is like the language found in the "holy war" aspects when Israel was first given the Promised Land. In Deuteronomy, enemies came together against God's people. The people prayed before they prepared their defense, and their own defenses were minor compared to the enemy. They had no real army, but Joshua reminds them that it doesnt matter because God is on their side.

We might wonder at the actions of these foreigners—after all, the Persian king ruled the land, and he had given Nehemiah authority to rebuild. But they are far from the Persian capital, and perhaps they thought they could get away with it.

Still, Nehemiah's authority and the language of holy war is *part* of his boldness. God had led him to believe the wall should be rebuilt; He had moved the king to grant Nehemiah the authority and given him resources; and once there, the work had progressed to the halfway point despite prior opposition. This all comes together

Does your passion match God's will? (Neh 4.9)

to give Nehemiah the conviction that what he is doing is God's work, and he will move ahead until God shows him otherwise.

For our purposes, Nehemiah always includes prayer at every stage and every crisis. *Because* it is not his passion, it is God's work.

Application

The concept of one's "passion" is popular today: "follow your passion," "find your passion," "it's my passion." Nehemiah had a passion, too: to protect God's people in Jerusalem and rebuild the wall. But as we have seen, he doesn't place his passion over God's will. He sought what God wanted—and if God had said, "no, stay, in Persia," Nehemiah would have stayed. He would not have argued, "But it's my passion!"

We see this same view here. The wall is making progress though there had been opposition. Each time, like here, Nehemiah stopped and sought God's direction and protection. Once he was sure, he moved ahead with concrete actions to fulfill the goal.

This is genuine Christian leadership. It does not seek its own goals, its own view of "how things need to be," its own "passion." God's will stands above all that. That means being constant in prayer, both in private and together with others.

Through our studies on prayer, we've read about many leaders of Israel who assumed they spoke for God, and acted without heeding or seeking Him first.

Some didn't care; others thought they already knew. Others prayed and "waited on the Lord."

Nehemiah's prayers cannot be divorced from his actions. While "waiting on the Lord" can be proper, sometimes we must act after the prayers are answered. When we engage in a project that we are passionate about we should first seek God's will on the matter (and be willing to give it up). Then we should continue to seek His will and take the human action necessary to make sure His will is done.

Surely Nehemiah was tempted to give up. He could have said, "these oppositions show that God wants me to stop." But he knew it was more complicated than that. Just because we meet difficulties does not mean it is not God's will.

Prayer is the avenue through which we seek God's will, seek His guidance, and gain the strength to act on it.

Are you aware of how you treat those who are different? (Neh 5.12-13)

And I called the priests, and made them take an oath to do as they had promised. I also shook out the fold of my garment and said, "So may God shake out everyone from house and from property who does not perform this promise. Thus may they be shaken out and emptied." And all the assembly said, "Amen," and praised the LORD.

The last prayer passage dealt with outside pressures and crises. This one addresses some internal problems having to do with the rich taking advantage of the poor. In a modern Western society that has no abject poverty, what can we learn from this prayer?

Background

The amount of rubble and garbage was slowing the repair of the wall, and so the scale of the task was causing the workers some disheartenment. Their families, worried for their safety, wanted them back home. Part of the problem was coming from the wives of the workers—since their husbands were off in Jerusalem having to work on the wall, they were responsible for everything having to do with their families. As they stretched out, it made things more difficult on them.

Three groups of people complain about the hardships—some leading to possible destitution, loans with high interest, and even selling their children as slaves!

Nehemiah became angry on hearing this. He calls the "nobles and the officials" to a public hearing, but his argument against them is less about the law and more about morality. Referring back to Jewish history, he notes that the Jewish people had been rescued from slavery and their debt-slavery redeemed—but these Jewish officials were putting their own brothers back in that situation! Second, Nehemiah points out how this must look to the other nations, and thus dishonors God. Finally, Nehemiah notes that he and his family have been part of the problem, too, for he is an official appointed by the Persian king himself.

He proposes two solutions to the other nobles and officials. First, he proposed that they should return any lands seized because of lack of payment due to the families—with no conditions. Second, he also urges the return of any interest collected on loans, and perhaps the cancellation of the loans themselves, or at least that such loans should cease in the future (v10).

The nobles and officials agree, and Nehemiah then shook out all the belongings he kept in his cloak, saying that if anyone went back on this pledge, God would "shake everything" from them. He made them take an oath to that effect—a vow.

The nobles and officials, and perhaps all the assembled people, did the same thing as a sign of their loyalty

Are you aware of how you treat those who are different? (Neh 5.12-13)

to the pledge. Their response is then to say Amen and praise God.

Meaning

The complaints appear to come from three different socio-economic groups. First, the families who owned no land were the hardest hit, because they had no income while the men were working on the wall. Since it was taking so long, they were in danger of becoming destitute (v2). Second, families who owned land, but had mortgaged it to nobles or officials to get through the difficult time. But, again, with it taking longer than expected, paying the mortgage was becoming difficult and were facing the sole option of selling their children as servants (hoping to redeem them later) or losing the land and becoming destitute (v3). The final group seems to be those who are landowners, too, but they do not have the assets or income to pay their taxes, so they are borrowing money in order to pay taxes (v4). Verse 5 seems to sum up the unfairness of this situation: while their husbands are doing the work to protect the city, the families super and the officials and nobles are unaffected.

This explains Nehemiah's anger—in the past, it was foreigners who enslaved God's people. But now it was their own leaders oppressing them! His solutions are simple and logical: make it easy on the people, it costs the officials almost nothing, and the city gains protection through the wall being built.

Note also that Nehemiah includes himself, which means he must have been a landowner and a noble too —not surprising since his family had been taken with the other nobles into Exile to Babylon. But taking some blame assuredly helped his case, for it portrayed the problem as a community problem, rather than only a problem with the rich. They were all in this together.

He then performed an act as part of the vow; not unusual in that time. People in the ancient world considered such acts as another way of solemnizing a vow or an agreement. People kept personal items in a fold of their robes, secured by a belt, serving much like our pockets do today. Nehemiah pulled the fold out and dumped his "pocket items" out onto the floor. The rest did likewise, and then followed with a "amen" to secure the vow, and then praised God.

Application

Disparity in wealth and status can sometimes cause big problems in a community. But what about congregations that do not have that sort economic variety (especially true in the West, where the kind of abject poverty that existed in the ancient world is no longer found). Are there other characteristics of Christian communities that have the same injustice against our own brothers and sisters, have-have-nots? Perhaps those who are "different" in some way: mentally challenged, drug or alcohol addicts, those with criminal records, or, in some areas, not being one of the "beautiful" people. Do we

Are you aware of how you treat those who are different? (Neh 5.12-13)

treat them separately? Do the church leaders? This would be especially applicable if theses people were doing the work of the church.

This passage also raises the question of physical wealth versus physical wealth. In modern society, which is fabulously well-off compared to the past, and tends towards materialism, we might focus far more on the physical needs, suggesting that it is not "fair" that some have more. Jesus fulfilled the *basic* physical needs of people (healing, feeding, etc.), but sought *primarily* to bring them to God. Studies show that, in general, the wealthy feel that their lives are less "meaningful" than those who just have enough to live on.[1]

When we turn to the prayer, we see that it is a prayer of praise (though it may include a vow and a curse, or at least, they are connected). What can we do with this prayer? First, we can examine our own views towards others who are "different." Often, we treat these people unjustly and are not even aware of it.[2] We can pray that God will open our eyes.

Second, we might consider the power of an accompanying act to prayer. As we have discussed in prior studies, actions such as kneeling, lying prostrate, or raising hands in prayer add to the meaning. But are there other, more specific acts you could take, depending on the

---

[1] For example, see the studies published by psychologist Roy Baumeister and others in 2013; that of psychologists Oishi and Dienter in *Psychological Science* in 2015. For a more popular treatment, see Gregg Easterbrook's book, *The Progress Paradox*.

[2] See James 2.1-13 for exhortations to be careful how we treat fellow believers who are different than us.

prayer you are offering. If you can think of some people you need to be treating more justly, is there an action you could add to the prayer to solemnize it—to make it more concrete to you? Make a vow to God, perform the act, then praise God for how he helps us listen, learn, and grow.

Praying about your past (Neh 5.19)

Remember for my good, O my God, all that I have done for this people.

This is such a short, simple prayer—yet one we all hope we could pray at the end of our lives. Nehemiah stands as one of the better examples of a faithful believer, and this prayer can serve as a goal for us.

Background

As we continue reading through Nehemiah, we learn that he was governor in Jerusalem for twelve years. Nehemiah tells the reader that he and his people did not use the food allowances that the governor's staff was due—unlike the previous governors, who demanded a lot of the people for their own good. He also acquired no lands for himself to increase his wealth or power. Instead, he focused on rebuilding the wall, as was his task.

He then describes one meal he would be expected to provide at an official dinner, which included the city officials and foreign dignitaries; again, he refused to tax the people for the food for such banquets, because he did not want to place a burden on the people.

The brief prayer above follows the listing of all the things he did. It simply asks God to remember him for all that he has done for the people.

Meaning

Just like in the last prayer passage, we see that this passage emphasizes that we should put the community of God's above the desires or wants of the individual. There are so many stories have we heard of church and faith organizations who live wealthy lives, far above the average person they serve. Power and status changes people. Both religious leaders and political leaders seem to forget they are to be servants of the people and begin to think of themselves too highly. Nehemiah focused on the *purpose* of his role—protecting God's people—and that helped him to remain grounded. Even in this short passage, he mentioned twice why he did things like he did: because of God.

The prayer itself is short and to the point. It is the first of six prayers that begin with "Remember...", and all seem to come near the end of his reign.[1] This seems to show that the people are not appreciative of the work he has done, and so he relies on God to remember his heart and his toil. In Nehemiah's previous prayers, he was in the middle of a narrative, engaged and passionate. These prayers are more reflective, looking back in time.

---

[1] See also 6:14; 13:14, 22, 29, 31, which we will explore later.

Note also that he is asking God to bless him for all his work. He knows that blessings only come from God; they do not come because we work hard, do good things, or are a "good person." God is the benefactor of all blessings.

Application

As believers, we should all be willing to sacrifice for the community of God's believers. Whether that be time, money, or something else (and perhaps it should be all of those), we should do so because (1) God has assigned it to us, and (2) we are to imitate Christ, as Christ imitates God, in caring for people.

The prayer is instructive. Our prayers usually concern "the moment at hand"—we ask for help or direction, we thank and praise Him for something, we intercede for others, or we confess and repent. But there is a place for reflective prayer when we look back a long distance into the past. For Nehemiah, it was to ask God to remember how much he had sacrifices and worked, even if others did not. It could be the same for us; or it might look back at less honorable actions. In the latter case, we can ask for forgiveness.

Such a prayer could also urge us on to good works now, so that, someday, we can look back on them and prayer Nehemiah's prayer!

Pray Continually and Do Your Job (Neh 6.9, 14)

But now, O God, strengthen my hands.
Remember Tobiah and Sanballat, O my God,
according to these things that they did, and
also the prophetess Noadiah and the rest of the
prophets who wanted to make me afraid.

What does a "life of prayer" mean? What does Paul mean when he wrote "pray continually"? Nehemiah's story presents an excellent example of one way to use prayer in our lives.

Background

Nehemiah's project is close to being finished. The wall is complete except for installing the gates. His adversaries, Sanballat, Tobiah, and Geshem had failed to stop him. But they aren't finished.

First, they send word for Nehemiah to come and meet them. But he knows they intend to harm him, so he refused. Three more times they ask, but he tells them he is too busy. Finally, they tell him that there are rumors that Nehemiah plans on rebelling once the wall is finished, and that he will set himself up as king. Nehemiah responds that he knows they are making up this story.

The first prayer above into his story—"But now, O God, strengthen my hands."

Their next ploy is to get him to enter the Temple, even into the holy of holies, under the guise of protection because his enemies want to kill him. But Nehemiah realized it was a set-up so they could accuse him of breaking the law by entering the Temple as a non-priest. He then inserts a second prayer into the story, asking God to remember what they all did.

Meaning

The first story is clear enough—a seemingly innocent invitation to meet, which, outside the city and his people, they could capture or even kill him. Nehemiah's response is to call them out on their deceit, but then to ask God to keep him strong.

However, there is a problem here that invites us to do a little deeper digging into the Hebrew text underlying the translation. The words "O God" are not there.[1] Literally, the phrase reads, "And now my hands are strengthened." These attempts are making him resolve even more to finish the wall. Why the translators wanted to make this a prayer is unclear.

The second story is more complex, involving a prophetess, a secret ally of Nehemiah's enemies, and

---

[1] So many translations add something like this. "O God" (NRSV, ASV, KJV, ESV); "I prayed" (NIV, NCV, The Message). The New Living Translation, however, has "So I continued to work with even greater determination."

Pray Continually and Do Your Job (Neh 6.9, 14)

the rule that only the priests could enter the center of the Temple (and only the High Priest into the Holy of Holies). Their plan is to tell him that a prophetess had a word from God that Nehemiah would be killed; therefore he should escape to the Temple to hide. Whether the plan was to kill him there, when he was alone in the Temple, or to put him in a bad light with the priests because he entered the Temple, is not clear.

Their story does not fool Nehemiah (and he has not seemed the type to run and hide). Once again, he refuses to go, and then offerers the second prayer above, asking God to remember those who plotted against him and his work. Note that this is another of the "Remember" prayers in Nehemiah.[2] Rather than taking things into his own hands, he leaves it to God—so he can get back to work on his calling to rebuild the wall.

Application

There are two things in this prayer that we can apply to our own prayers. First, note how, as Nehemiah tells his story, he inserts prayers here and there (even though the first one is not a prayer, he does this in other places). We should seek to have a life of prayer that is in frequent communication with God—not only in formal situations where we "take time to pray," but also just in the course of our day, like we might speak to a constant

---

[2] See also 5.19; 13:14, 22, 29, 31.

companion. This is probably what Paul meant when he wrote "pray continually" in 1 Thessalonians 5.17.

The second lesson is the more difficult. Anyone who seeks to do God's will in life will encounter obstacles. It may not be people trying to harm you, but it could come in the form of blocking your actions, access, or processes. To stop you from doing the work you are called to do. Maybe you are ostracized from a certain group. Or it might come in the form of ridicule and belittlement. The reaction of Nehemiah is sound: ignore to the best of your ability, get back to work, and ask God to take care of them. We need not spend time fighting or worrying about those who work against God's plans.

If Nehemiah can do this in the face of physical danger, surely we can do so in the face of less.

Renewing your faith through prayer and physical acts (Neh 8.6)

Then Ezra blessed the LORD, the great God, and all the people answered, "Amen, Amen," lifting up their hands. Then they bowed their heads and worshiped the LORD with their faces to the ground.

How do you keep your faith strong and consistent? How do you avoid complacency that comes to all of us. Ezra and the people of Israel have an idea: taking the reading of scripture seriously through prayer and physical acts and gestures.

Background

Once the wall was finished, the author of Nehemiah treats us to a long list of names of the returning exiles (7.4-73). We then read three chapters about the spiritual renewal of the people. The section begins with a "covenant renewal," which began with of a reading of the Law of Moses to the whole community of people in Jerusalem. This reading came at the request of the people: they had a desire for spiritual renewal. Moreover, it was not done at the Temple precincts, but in a common place in the city (the public square before the Water Gate).

What you might notice immediately upon beginning this chapter is that the person leading the ceremony is Nehemiah, but Ezra. These three chapters (8-10) sound more like they belong in the book of Ezra in chapters 7-10. But the work of Ezra and Nehemiah were not separate; they overlapped, and both worked on restoring Jerusalem and the people of God to their true position. And so this section fits well as an introduction to the rest of Nehemiah after chapter 10.

Before he began reading the Law of Moses, Ezra offered a blessing upon God. The people responded with "Amen," raised their hands, and bowed their heads in worship.

Following the reading (or perhaps during it), priests and others were present with Ezra, to explain and interpret the law for the people when they did not understand. As they listened and learned what attitude, actions, and requirements there were, they began to cry.

Meaning

There are some important issues to explore in this passage relating to prayer.

This was not the first covenant renewal that the Jewish people had held. They had been done periodically throughout the history of Israel after times of difficulty and neglect of their faith.

Renewing your faith through prayer and physical acts (Neh 8.6)

Offering a blessing (a benediction) before the reading of Scripture occurs as far back as we have records of the reading of God's Word. So this prayer, at this time, is not unusual. It is a brief and simple expression, maybe just "Blessed be the great God!" or "Blessed be our God, the great one!" The people's response may have been a custom, too. First, they shout "Amen! Amen!" which means "so be it!" Then, they raise their hands to God as a sign of reaching to him, praising him, and blessings him. Finally, they prostrate themselves as a sign of their humble adoration of God and their understanding of the seriousness of the reading.

As the people listened and understood, they saw that they had not been "walking the talk" or "practicing what they preached." It cut them to the heart, and they wept. It is as if they were told, "You have been saved by God—now go live like it!" and they felt like hypocrites who had received a gift and then ignored both the gift and the Giver.

Faith in God is not a belief (though belief is the root of faith), it is action and attitude in life. It determines what we do, how we treat people, how we work, and how we play. In the modern world, it is tempting to divorce theory and practice. We see it from our political leaders, our community leaders, our entertainers, and even our religious leaders. We often say the right things but fail to live them out. Believing means nothing with actions that flow from that belief.

Application

Bricks and mortar (or a church building) might be necessary for the people of God to have a safe, physical place for worship, but it is not enough. In fact, they are meaningless without public and unified dedication to God and what is required of us to be His people.

Are we as happy to hear the Word of God as these ancient followers? They *asked* for it. Do we sit in boredom as we listen to it read? Or do we listen with great attention, to see what we can learn and what calls us to account—perhaps even for tears to come to our eyes as we realize that we have not lived as thankfully as we should? That we have not lived disciplined lives of faith in response to the blessings God gave us.

For those of us who have spent many decades as believers, and listen to the same passages over and over, it may be difficult for our minds to drift. But it is part of what we are called to do—seek new words, new meanings. It must also be said that our leaders (and those reading) should help us hear the words anew, to help call us out when we need it, and to explain it to us. They also fall short.

When we attend to a reading of the Bible with these actions and attitudes, then it becomes clear why a blessing upon God is appropriate at the beginning. The texts are not *just* stories, *just* commandments, *just* song. The words have power, imparted by God, that can speak anew each time to generations, families, and individuals, every time we hear them. Such powerful words re-

Renewing your faith through prayer and physical acts (Neh 8.6)

quire a serious approach, and the first part of that is beginning with prayer before we read.

Try this today: choose a selection from the Bible to read (it could be Nehemiah 8, if you wish). Offer a brief blessing upon God before, raise your hands, and then prostrate yourself before you begin your reading.

How to offer a prayer of confession, Part 1 (Neh 9.3-5)

> *"Stand up and bless the LORD your God from everlasting to everlasting. Blessed be your glorious name, which is exalted above all blessing and praise."*

Most of us were never taught how to offer a prayer of confession, though we were probably told we should. In one sense, it seems easy: "I committed this wrong, and it is my fault." But what if our wrongdoing has been long; what if it was a way of life? What if we want a deeper and more encompassing confession as part of a spiritual renewal? Nehemiah 9 shows us how.

Background

After they finished the wall, the people came together for a covenant renewal ceremony, and a blessing was offered before the reading of scripture (the Law of Moses). The people wept when they heard how unfaithful they had been, but Nehemiah and Ezra told them it was no time to weep, but to go and rejoice in the day of the Lord.

They came back the next to to study the word of God again. Learning about the Festival of Booths, a commemoration of when the Israelites wandered in the desert, they celebrated it right then for seven days—a time of remembering how God cared for them, guided them, and sustained them.

The next prayer is a lengthy confession—appropriate when people want to renew their faith. Because it is so long, we will explore it in several parts.

We begin here, with the people wearing sackcloth, putting dirt on their heads, and fasting. The text tells us they spend a fourth of the day hearing the word of God read, and another fourth confessing their sins. Ezra will offer a prayer of confession for all the people—for all of Israel and her ancestors—but first, he begins with a blessing.

Meaning

Sackcloth is a coarse animal skin, usually from a black goat. Not made as smooth and finished as other clothes, it was uncomfortable and unattractive. Donning it was a common sign of mounting or repentance (not only among Israelites).

Many physical acts accompany prayer in the Bible: standing, kneeling, prostrate, arms out, arms up, etc. But to bless and praise God, standing is appropriate as a sign of respect. So Ezra tells the people to stand up and bless God. "Blessed be your glorious name" is the beginning, often found in prayers of blessing.

"From everlasting to everlasting" is a phrase that tries to capture the unending characteristic of God's existence. "From forever to forever," or, we might say, "for ever and ever." He has always been and always will be present.

The last phrase is a common Jewish and Christian phrase that sends a clear message of belief—God is unique among all beings in the universe and in existence. Whether other gods, spiritual beings, or angels existed or not, it did not matter to believers—God is unique above all else.

Application

There are a few things we can learn from this first part of a prayer of confession. Again, this is not a simple prayer that confesses a wrong—it is part of a ceremony of a renewal of faith. So it is longer and more involved. Still, we can use some of these ideas in even our shorter prayers of confession, and not just when we feel called to a more complete spiritual renewal.

First, note the physical acts. Perhaps, before confessing, you could put on some clothing to set the tone. Finding sackcloth might be difficult, but any old pair of uncomfortable clothes should do. Anything that implies poverty and discomfort to symbolize the poverty and discomfort of your faith. They put dirt on their heads—perhaps we do not shower or wash the entire day as a symbol of our spiritual uncleanness. They also fasted, probably for the whole day.

Most important, don't begin with the prayer of confession (which is about you), but start by blessing God (making it about Him). God should be the center of all we do—we are secondary. Begin with Him, and then move to us and our needs.

How to offer a prayer of confession, Part 2 (Neh 9.6-11)

And Ezra said: "You are the LORD, you alone; you have made heaven, the heaven of heavens, with all their host, the earth and all that is on it, the seas and all that is in them. To all of them you give life, and the host of heaven worships you. You are the LORD, the God who chose Abram and brought him out of Ur of the Chaldeans and gave him the name Abraham; and you found his heart faithful before you, and made with him a covenant to give to his descendants the land of the Canaanite, the Hittite, the Amorite, the Perizzite, the Jebusite, and the Girgashite; and you have fulfilled your promise, for you are righteous.

"And you saw the distress of our ancestors in Egypt and heard their cry at the Red Sea. You performed signs and wonders against Pharaoh and all his servants and all the people of his land, for you knew that they acted insolently against our ancestors. You made a name for yourself, which remains to this day. And you divided the sea before them, so that they passed through the sea on dry land, but you threw their

pursuers into the depths, like a stone into mighty waters.

We might often think of a prayer of confession as simple: "I confess my sin of pride, O God." That is appropriate, of course. But perhaps confession should sometimes help us answer questions such as "Why should we confess our wrongdoing?" "Why should we confess it to God?" This prayer of confession begins with praise to remind us *why* confession matters, bringing power to our confession that might not exist otherwise.

Background

The last prayer began this lengthy confession with sackcloth and ashes, and a prayer that blessed God, placing the focus on *Him* first, even though the prayer of confession that follows is about the people. Genuine confession can only come when we know who God is in all his power and glory, and that is where this part of the prayer begins.

The prayer begins like a hymn: a call to praise God. How do they praise God? By describing and glorifying Him as creator and as the giver of life. For the Jews assembled in this story, the history of their people is also a reason to praise God: He is the one who chose their ancestor Abraham and brought him safely to the promised land; He is the one who made a covenant—a promise—that it would be their land for many generations. The praise then turns to how God delivered them from slavery in Egypt.

How to offer a prayer of confession, Part 2 (Neh 9.6-11)

Note that the last part of the praise does something that might seem unusual to us: it describes how God, by doing all these things, "made a name for himself."

Meaning

This is a prayer of confession, but it begins with this lengthy praise first, as we noted above. Confession should begin with praise. While many praise prayers are simple ("I praise your name, God") this one goes into more detail about why God should be praised.

He is the One who created everything, and that makes Him unique in all existence, and therefore worthy of praise: "you alone are Yahweh." The complexity and beauty of creation is unparalleled, and therefore, He is worthy of praise for that.

But he also takes actions to benefit his creation, and, and so it is proper to praise him for those actions. Praise prayers in the Bible often use historical events as a reason for praise (for example see Ps 78; 105; 135; 136). The choice of Abram and his descendants was an act of blessing and mercy, because the world would be blessed through them in many ways (in this case, through Abraham's ancestor Joseph who predicted widespread famine and helped Egypt and the surrounding lands to stock up in order to survive). He gave them a promise and gave them land—also to be praised. When they forgot about him and cried out in slavery in Egypt, He kept his promise and delivered them back to the promised land; another historical reason He should be praised.

So this prayer of confession begins with a detailed praise of God. Why should we confess our wrongdoing? Why should we confess it to God? Because of who He is and what he has done. Beginning a prayer of confession with praise reminds us *why* confession matters.

All of these reasons for praise have to do with God's grace and goodness towards his people—an important characteristic for people who are seeking forgiveness through confession. He is the Creator, the Promise-Maker, and the Savior—all reasons why we should seek to praise Him and also to confess our wrongdoing to Him.

Application

Since we are exploring this prayer of confession in five sections, we have not arrived at our confession yet. The beginning is a detailed praise prayer, and as such, can stand as a model for that kind of prayer.

Sometimes we don't think much about praising God—the closest we might get it thanking him for something he has done. While praise and thanksgiving are connected and similar, they are different. Praise is about who God is. Note that every reason for praise has something to do with his *character*—he is a creative God, a life-giving God, a promise-keeping God, and a God who saves.

How to offer a prayer of confession, Part 2 (Neh 9.6-11)

Plan out a prayer of praise based on this model. Keep in mind that you are headed toward a confession of wrongdoing. Today, work on the praise that gives you the reasons why you will confess as we continue. Structure it in three parts: God as creator, God as one who acts in history, and God as a gracious savior.

How can you praise God for creation? What things come to mind: mountains, the sea, a newborn child or grandchild, etc. Let that be the first part of your prayer. Then, turn to historical events. What things has God done in the past that showed his graciousness or resulted in grace to you? It could be as simple as where you were born, or the family you were born into, or an opportunity to be part of a particular community, or even your educational or vocational opportunities. Of course, it could also include the choosing of Abraham and the Jews, which also led to the birth of Jesus and the salvation on the cross. Organize these gracious acts in the past into a praise like the one above.

Finally, consider the times God has shown forgiveness grace when you did not deserve it. What has he delivered you from? It could be something medical, or emotional, or family-oriented, or perhaps based on your wrongdoing. The focus here, though, is not on those sufferings or punishments, but on God's deliverance from them.

Write this prayer down, either as an outline or word-for-word. Offer it as your prayer for today. You can use it later as an introduction to a prayer of confession as we explore this prayer more.

How to offer a prayer of confession, Part 3 (Neh 9.12-25)

Moreover, you led them by day with a pillar of cloud, and by night with a pillar of fire, to give them light on the way in which they should go. You came down also upon Mount Sinai, and spoke with them from heaven, and gave them right ordinances and true laws, good statutes and commandments, and you made known your holy sabbath to them and gave them commandments and statutes and a law through your servant Moses. For their hunger you gave them bread from heaven, and for their thirst you brought water for them out of the rock, and you told them to go in to possess the land that you swore to give them.

"But they and our ancestors acted presumptuously and stiffened their necks and did not obey your commandments; they refused to obey, and were not mindful of the wonders that you performed among them; but they stiffened their necks and determined to return to their slavery in Egypt. But you are a God ready to forgive, gracious and merciful, slow to anger and abounding in steadfast love, and you did not forsake them. Even when they had cast an

image of a calf for themselves and said, 'This is your God who brought you up out of Egypt,' and had committed great blasphemies, you in your great mercies did not forsake them in the wilderness; the pillar of cloud that led them in the way did not leave them by day, nor the pillar of fire by night that gave them light on the way by which they should go. You gave your good spirit to instruct them, and did not withhold your manna from their mouths, and gave them water for their thirst. Forty years you sustained them in the wilderness so that they lacked nothing; their clothes did not wear out and their feet did not swell. And you gave them kingdoms and peoples, and allotted to them every corner, so they took possession of the land of King Sihon of Heshbon and the land of King Og of Bashan. You multiplied their descendants like the stars of heaven, and brought them into the land that you had told their ancestors to enter and possess. So the descendants went in and possessed the land, and you subdued before them the inhabitants of the land, the Canaanites, and gave them into their hands, with their kings and the peoples of the land, to do with them as they pleased. And they captured fortress cities and a rich land, and took possession of houses filled with all sorts of goods, hewn cisterns, vineyards, olive orchards, and fruit trees in abundance; so they

How to offer a prayer of confession, Part 3 (Neh 9.12-25)

ate, and were filled and became fat, and delighted themselves in your great goodness.

Prayers of confession should be grounded in the character of God: creative, gracious, compassionate, and patient. Part three of this prayer of confession shows us how to build a prayer of confession that is deep, wide, and meaningful.

Background

The third part of this prayer continues praising God by reciting how God provided for the Israelites while they were wandering in the desert. Not only did he deliver them from Egypt, as described in part two of our study of this prayer, but he gave them food (manna), water, and shelter—often in miraculous ways.

How do the people respond? With selfishness, refusal to follow God's directions, and stubbornness. At one point, they even told Moses that they were better off in slavery in Egypt! Worse still, they created an idol to worship and ascribed their delivery to a golden calf. God had freed them, protected them, fed them, and guided them for forty years. Despite their ungratefulness, he them into a great nation of people, conquered lands for them, given them fertile soils, and made them successful, prosperous, and happy. All because God is good.

Meaning

This section continues describing the great graciousness of God but introduces the first element of why confession is necessary. Amid describing God's protection for forty years in the wilderness, the prayer recalls how the people whined, complained, failed to follow God's ways, and rebelled against Him. The reason for noting the unfaithfulness is not only to cite the need for confession, but also to show that despite that past rebellion, God continued to be gracious: he brought them into the Promised Land, helped them defeat their enemies, and made them prosperous.

The confession began with praise of who God is—his character and his great acts of creation and choosing of his people. It continues here with a recitation of his care, nurturing and protection. Then, despite the failure of people to follow Him, he still kept his promises to them and gave them great blessings. All of this is background to set up the need and purpose of the subsequent confession: begin with God, His power and majesty, his great acts in history, and his overwhelming graciousness and patience.

Application

As we have seen before in all these studies, the prayer types need not stand alone. Not only can they be used together in one prayer, but they can connect and interact with each other. Here, we see praise and thankfulness

How to offer a prayer of confession, Part 3 (Neh 9.12-25)

for God's graciousness helps set the tone of the prayer for *why* we need to confess our wrongdoing (because he is gracious and we rebel) and that He *is* the sort of God who has incredible patience (long-suffering).

For the moment, a prayer of confession need not end with you asking for anything. After all, confessing is just that: confession alone. A petition for forgiveness can come later, but there is nothing wrong with a mere prayer that tells God the facts.

Offer a prayer today in which you recite times when God has been gracious or generous to you, but you have not bee grateful. You might begin the prayer with praising God as Creator, then for the things he has done for you, and then how you had acted ungratefully. Beyond that, tell Him how He has continued to be faithful even when you have not.

How does it feel to end a prayer there? We often end our prayers by asking God for something (or the entire prayer is only a petition). What is it like to just acknowledge God's graciousness and then your own unfaithfulness, with no requests?

How to offer a prayer of confession, Part 4 (Neh 9.26-31)

"Nevertheless they were disobedient and rebelled against you and cast your law behind their backs and killed your prophets, who had warned them in order to turn them back to you, and they committed great blasphemies. Therefore you gave them into the hands of their enemies, who made them suffer. Then in the time of their suffering they cried out to you and you heard them from heaven, and according to your great mercies you gave them saviors who saved them from the hands of their enemies. But after they had rest, they again did evil before you, and you abandoned them to the hands of their enemies, so that they had dominion over them; yet when they turned and cried to you, you heard from heaven, and many times you rescued them according to your mercies. And you warned them in order to turn them back to your law. Yet they acted presumptuously and did not obey your commandments, but sinned against your ordinances, by the observance of which a person shall live. They turned a stubborn shoulder and stiffened their neck and would not obey. Many years you were patient with them,

> *and warned them by your spirit through your prophets; yet they would not listen. Therefore you handed them over to the peoples of the lands. Nevertheless, in your great mercies you did not make an end of them or forsake them, for you are a gracious and merciful God.*

Have you ever had enough of someone's selfishness or mistreatment of them that you said, "no more!" Or perhaps you withdrew for a time, hoping they would learn, and they did, only to return to their selfish ways? How many times would you put up with this? How much would be enough to say, "never again"? For God, the answer is never, as shown in this prayer of confession.

Background

We are now in the fourth part of this long prayer, the last section before it closes in verses 32-37. This prayer of confession began with everything *but* confession: a praise of God, a description of *why* God should be praised, and then reminders of specific things God has done for the people. This sets up why they need to confess—it grounds the confession in the character of God. Now, the prayer is ready to reveal *why* confession is necessary. Recall why this prayer is being offered: the people have returned to their land after 80+ years, and have just refinished building the wall of Jerusalem, and are beginning to renew their dedication to God. But their past requires confession.

How to offer a prayer of confession, Part 4 (Neh 9.26-31)

They ignored God's laws, they killed the prophets he sent to teach and warn them, they insulted God in significant ways. After much patience and many chances, God allowed their enemies to conquer them. But God heard their cries for help, and he saved them through a leader. They thanked God and followed him for a short time. But after a time, they returned back to the same self-centered lifestyles as before. So they were conquered again…and the cycle repeated: they ignored God, they were captured, they cried out to Him, He saved them. This section of the prayer ends with a line reminding them of why God keeps doing it: "Nevertheless, in your great mercies you did not make an end of them or forsake them, for you are a gracious and merciful God."

Meaning

If you studied the prayers of Judges with us, this recitation of the sins of God's people would sound familiar—the cycle of rebellion-suffering-prayer-deliverance is emphasized there.[1] Rather than focusing on any specific event, though, this prayer addresses with the nature of the people to rebel against God and His response.

The structure is interesting, too. The prayer mentions three times that the people were rebelled and then conquered (26-27a; 28a; 29-30). The first two times, the prayer tells how God had compassion and delivered

---

[1] See Judg 2:11–23, see also 2 Kgs 17.

them. But the third time does not. Why? Probably because it is referencing the Babylonian exile, which was still going on, even though some of the Jews had been allowed to return to Jerusalem.

There is a strong sense here that to reject the Law (the Law of Moses) is the same as denying God. Perhaps this is not surprising, because the Law was God's way of telling His people "here is how you should live for the best life as I created it."

How can this be applied to the time after Christ, where followers of God no longer live under the Law? Paul's explanations in Galatians 3-5 are instructive. He writes that the Law is still in effect, but rather than a set of rules to try to follow, it is fulfilled by living "in Christ" with the help of the Spirit. Sacrifices are no longer necessary because Jesus was the Universal Sacrifice for all time. But the manner of how a believer should live is the same. Acting with "the love of Christ" [2] and living *becuase* you are saved will result in the same actions as living under the law: you won't murder, you won't betray, you won't covet, you won't steal, and so on. But instead of trying *not* to do something (follow the rules), we live "in Christ" and so, by living like him, we fulfill all the law.

> *...the fruit of the Spirit is love, joy, peace, patience, kindness, generosity, faithfulness, gentleness, and self-control. There is no law against such things. And those who belong to*

---

[2] Gal 5.14.

How to offer a prayer of confession, Part 4 (Neh 9.26-31)

Christ Jesus have crucified the flesh with its passions and desires. If we live by the Spirit, let us also be guided by the Spirit. (Gal 5.22-25)

So disobedience for a Christian is a failure to live in Christ and actions that come from it: self-centeredness, judgmentalism, lack of compassion, and so on (the opposites of the list Paul gives above).

Application

There are two key elements in this prayer that we can use in our own prayers of confession. The first is to see how we have disobeyed God by not living in a Christ-like manner. The second is to take joy in God's response—no matter how badly we turn away from Him, and how many times we do it, He is ready to forgive us and wipe the slate clean, because He is a compassionate God. *That* should lead us back to living a grateful and Christ-like life.

Try this: using the prayer passage above, rewrite it from a Christian point of view, substituting "Christ-like," "in Christ," "the Spirit," (or whatever works) for the Law. Make other changes as needed to fit your circumstance. Then offer the prayer of confession as your own, remembering that God's great compassion and patience is a reason to rejoice and praise Him.

How to offer a prayer of confession, Part 5 (Neh 9.32-37)

"Now therefore, our God—the great and mighty and awesome God, keeping covenant and steadfast love—do not treat lightly all the hardship that has come upon us, upon our kings, our officials, our priests, our prophets, our ancestors, and all your people, since the time of the kings of Assyria until today. You have been just in all that has come upon us, for you have dealt faithfully and we have acted wickedly; our kings, our officials, our priests, and our ancestors have not kept your law or heeded the commandments and the warnings that you gave them. Even in their own kingdom, and in the great goodness you bestowed on them, and in the large and rich land that you set before them, they did not serve you and did not turn from their wicked works. Here we are, slaves to this day—slaves in the land that you gave to our ancestors to enjoy its fruit and its good gifts. Its rich yield goes to the kings whom you have set over us because of our sins; they have power also over our bodies and over our livestock at their pleasure, and we are in great distress."

Background

We finally come to the end of the long prayer of confession. As we noted previously, this long prayer is an excellent example of how a prayer can include different prayer types: this one began with praise before it turned to confession. Having grounded the prayer in God, it then turned to the confession itself. But it does not end there. It closes with an intercession, a cry for God to respond to the confession, and so ends on a note of hope.

Meaning

Even though the confession closes with an intercession, the beginning of it harkens back to the praise at the beginning of the long prayer "the great and mighty and awesome God, keeping covenant and steadfast love." It then turns right to the intercession by asking Him to take account of their suffering for so long—since the time of the Assyrians in the 6th century BC! The intercession admits that their suffering and punishment was just—but closes with "we are in great distress," calling for God to practice mercy and grace, just as he practices judgment.

Note that the structure of this last section matches the structure of the entire prayer: praise, confession, intercession. This is not by accident, of course. Repeating something emphasizes it, and the number three also served to emphasize.

How to offer a prayer of confession, Part 5 (Neh 9.32-37)

There are also a number of key words and themes interspersed throughout this section of the prayer, also emphasizing the confession: the wicked acts of God's people, ignorance of His laws, rejection of warnings, but also the gift of the land, enjoyment of its fruits, covenant, God's justice, God's grace.

This prayer is a long, thought out, well-written prayer of confession. It does not simply confess the sins, but places the sin in the larger context through the use of praise and intercession. As we come to God to confess our sins, we recognize that it is the greatness of the power of God that makes our actions wrong—and also that He is the One who can wipe our guilt away. The confession itself *names* the sins—it is not enough simply to say "I have sinned" when the sin is so deep and lengthy. Finally, the intercession recognizes that God cares about his people—punishment is not the final word.

Application

A prayer of confession is a somber and sad affair. It admits to living outside of God's purposes, of hurting others, and of living as if *we* are God—usurping the King of the Universe from His rightful place! Such a betrayal deserves death in many earthly and spiritual realms. This reality makes confession a terrible but necessary part of prayer.

Yet this confession shows that it need not begin and end there. With confession comes hope. Because God is great and mighty, because He can do anything, and because His nature is to be gracious and forgiving…there is a hopeful note. So a confession can remember God's greatness and generosity, and can, after confession, ask for him to extend mercy, if it is His will.

We should take hope in our own sins and confess them. The Israelites had committed terrible sins against God, and had done it for centuries, in spite of his great gift of land and its prosperity. They ignored him, lived selfish lives, enslaved their owner people and even put some to death, and worshipped other Gods. Yet he forgave them when they confessed. He not only forgave, but he also restored them to their land and fortune and gave them a fresh start. All was forgiven.

Confession is a crucial step towards remaining and reclaiming our relationship with God. Many of us do not offer confessions often enough: we focus on requests and thanksgivings. But a relationship that only asks and thanks is not a deep relationship.

Today, think about some way or ways that you have usurped God from his role. Perhaps you have lived outside your created purpose: treated others as less than God would, engaged in unhealthy behavior (physical, emotional, or spiritual), or just ignored God. Write down a prayer of confession modeled on this one (either an outline or fully written). Begin with praise, remembering that He is your Sovereign King. Confess the wrongdoing, with specifics. Then, petition him, based on his compassion and grace, to forgive you and show you a better way.

How to offer a prayer of confession, Part 5 (Neh 9.32-37)

Think about how a prayer, structured in this way, is different from just a prayer that only confesses.

Bringing Together the Past and the Present in Your Prayers (Neh 12.24)

And the leaders of the Levites: Hashabiah, Sherebiah, and Jeshua son of Kadmiel, with their associates over against them, to praise and to give thanks, according to the commandment of David the man of God, section opposite to section. Mattaniah, Bakbukiah, Obadiah, Meshullam, Talmon, and Akkub were gatekeepers standing guard at the storehouses of the gates.

Background

After the long prayer of confession in chapter 9, the writer of Nehemiah treats us to a lengthy list of the names of signatories to the agreement to restore their community to the ways of God. This includes not only a list of names, clans, and official groups (10.1-28), but the specifics of *how* they will follow the law of God (10.29-39).

Next comes a list of people who will move into the city (selected by a lottery), followed by a list of people in various settlements and then lists of other groups, such as the priests (11.1-12.26). It is in this section that we find the next mention of prayer.

The leader of the Levites and their associates are to "praise and give thanks" in song, as ordered by King David.

Meaning

The prayers here, praise and thanksgiving, are offered in song, as commanded by David (found in places in First and Second Chronicles, see for example 1 Chron 15–16; 23–29).The groups are to do it by standing opposite one another in their section, and singing antiphonally, that is, the two choirs interact with one another, singing alternate musical prayers.

The writer here has brought together the past and present in this explanation: the restoration of the religious practices of the current believer with what was done in the past. This connects the past practices to the present, giving weight and meaning to what they are doing. It helps avoid a more modern method of coming up with practices of prayer, singing, and worship that ignores the past practices. Not that contemporary worship shouldn't consider modern styles, but when it ignores what has been done in the past, it cuts itself off from the rich practice of prayer and singing (and worship in general).

Trying to "modernize" worship to attract people is fine, but any "new way" must explore and understand how it was done throughout the ages, to remain true to

Bringing Together the Past and the Present in Your Prayers (Neh 12.24)

the meaning. Otherwise, worship becomes subject to the tyranny of the moment, frequently shifting style and meaning, which caused it to lose its grounding.

Judaism and Christianity are beliefs that are grounded in historical events: God created the world; He chose a people; He showed them how to live the best life; He punished and restored them; He sent his Messiah, and so on. A faith system built on historical events that ignores the MEANING of those events becomes pablum —worship that is disconnected from its anchor in all but words, drifting upon waters of shallow meaning that do not satisfy the deeper longings of our souls.

It is not always easy to find a balance between the deep traditions of our faith and modern styles and interests. Paul himself dealt with this in trying to present the Gospel message to the Gentiles (1 Cor 9). But rooting our practice of prayer in the past is crucial for it to remain meaningful and effective.

Application

Consider your practice of prayer and its larger context of worship. How might your practice of prayer have been influenced by modern practice and cultural emphases? In what way has this been negative? In what ways is it positive?

Are there times in prayer where you have been excited to try something new, only to find later it lacking once the newness wore off? Do you find any comfort in praying ancient prayers, knowing that other believers, just like you, have been praying them for thousands of years all over the world?

Offer a prayer *about* prayer, asking God to help you find a practice and a meaning in prayer true to the past traditions, while still relevant to modern sensibilities.

Adding Joy and Physical Acts to Your Prayers (Neh 12.27, 31, 42, 46)

Now at the dedication of the wall of Jerusalem they sought out the Levites in all their places, to bring them to Jerusalem to celebrate the dedication with rejoicing, with thanksgivings and with singing, with cymbals, harps, and lyres.

Then I brought the leaders of Judah up onto the wall, and appointed two great companies that gave thanks and went in procession.

And the singers sang with Jezrahiah as their leader.

For in the days of David and Asaph long ago there was a leader of the singers, and there were songs of praise and thanksgiving to God.

We often offer prayers at the beginning of events or projects. We might usually pray a thanksgiving at the end. But here, the end of a project calls for exuberant and joyful singing of prayers! The prayers are also connected with physical acts of walking around the city.

What can we take from these prayers to use in our own practice?

Background

The four mentions of prayer in this passage are part of the climax of the life of Nehemiah: the dedication of the city wall. Two groups of people made a procession each, then went out the gate in opposite directions, offering thanksgiving prayers along the way. Halfway around the city, they entered and joined together, standing at the rebuilt Temple for a service of praise and thanks. As we have seen before, singing and music is a significant part of the celebration, and prayers can be sung as well as spoken—especially prayers of praise and thanksgiving, as we see here.

But the important final note connects the present celebration to the past when these worship services were held regularly and often.

Meaning

The two processions began on the west of the city, near the Valley Gate to the top of the wall. The first group went south (counterclockwise) on the top of the wall, all the way to to the Water Gate opposite the Valley Gate. Along the way, the choir sang or spoke thanksgiving prayers to God. There, they left the wall and headed to the Temple.

Adding Joy and Physical Acts to Your Prayers (Neh 12.27, 31, 42, 46)

The second group followed Nehemiah from the Valley gate, along the top of the wall clockwise to the Sheep Gate. Along the way, they also sang or spoke thanksgiving prayers to God. From there, they descended from the wall and headed to the Temple.

Each group traveled about two-thirds of a mile around the city, to re-enter and become one group at the Temple. What is the meaning of these processions? They are a celebration of the completed work. Traveling *on* the wall to celebrate the wall. We can imagine that, as they walked, each person in each group might have seen part of the way they had worked on. It was now complete—despite the troubles from outside and inside. That was a reason to offer thanksgiving to God.

Notice how often the element of "joy" is mentioned in the prayers and in the entire passage—"with rejoicing" at the beginning (v 27) and then especially at verse 43:

> *They offered great sacrifices that day and **rejoiced**, for God had made them **rejoice** with great **joy**; the women and children also **rejoiced**. The **joy** of Jerusalem was heard far away.*

What an intense focus on the joy of this occasion! The emphasis on joy parallels the same emphasis on joy when they finished rebuilding the temple (see Ezra 6.16–22). Some might see faith as a way of life that involves following rules, asking for guidance, and giving thanks when something good happens. But we should not forget the joy permeates a life lived with God—He rejoiced when he finished creation in Genesis, and heaven rejoices at the end in Revelation. In between, despite struggles, hardships, and loss, there is always joy to in God (see also Rom. 5:2-5; 8:18-25; Heb. 12:2).

Application

What can we learn about prayer from this joyful passage? First, prayer comes at the beginning and during our events and projects. Perhaps those are petitions and intercessions for perseverance and good work. But we should never forget the importance of joyful prayer at the end of tasks, events, and projects. It is not only a time for thanksgiving that it is finished, but also praise and joy!

Second, consider the physical acts that can accompany this prayer-filled joy. Not only did they pray and sing, for they walked around the very wall they had just finished.

One aspect of the ancient Greco-Roman world-view is the separation between the physical and the spiritual. They are two different things that don't have a lot of overlap. We have inherited that view in the modern world, but it is not found in scripture. The physical world, created by God, is completely intertwined with the spiritual. God created the universe with his being. He led the Israelites by fire and clouds. He was present in the physical Tabernacle, and then in the Temple. His Son, the Messiah, was a physical being. The life God

Adding Joy and Physical Acts to Your Prayers (Neh 12.27, 31, 42, 46)

gives us is sustained daily by Him and the world He crested.

When we separate the two, as the Greeks and Romans did, it makes it easy to place the spiritual to one side—on Sundays, or in worship, or set apart in "devotional" times. Then we got out to the "physical" world and focus on materialism.

Consider how you might incorporate prayer more into your daily life: family, work, friends, errands, and more. Think about how you might use prayer at the end of events, and how you might incorporate a more physical aspect into prayer.

Asking God to Remember You (Neh 13.14, 22)

Remember me, O my God, concerning this, and do not wipe out my good deeds that I have done for the house of my God and for his service.

And I commanded the Levites that they should purify themselves and come and guard the gates, to keep the sabbath day holy. Remember this also in my favor, O my God, and spare me according to the greatness of your steadfast love.

Background

Both of these prayers, similar in content and structure, come from this last chapter of Nehemiah—a chapter that is more sobering than the previous. The prayer comes during events about 15 years later than in the last prayer passage

Nehemiah, back in Persia after his first term, asks the king if he can return to Jerusalem to see how things are going. The king grants him a second term as governor. When he arrives, he finds that many of the reforms he instituted have failed. The people have forgotten, or ignored, or simply let them lapse. Most have to do with the maintenance and care of those who work in the Temple and the keeping of the Sabbath. Another issue (which we'll examine in the next chapter), is making sure that the community of believers are not influenced by foreign practices and religion.

The first prayer comes after Nehemiah discovered that the Levites and the singers of the Temple were not being given the donations of food meant for them (to support them so they could do the work). Therefore, they had gone back to laboring on farms. Angry, Nehemiah confronted the officials, and then put others in charge of the donations—those he deemed more responsible and faithful. The section closes with his short prayer above: that God remember all the good things he did for God's house.

Next (vv15-22), he discovers that food sellers and artisans were bringing goods into the city on the Sabbath to sell to next day, and that some foreigners (non-Jews) were selling on the Sabbath. This violated the law of Moses and part of Nehemiah's significant reforms. The Sabbath was a day devoted to rest and worship—carrying burdens and working was forbidden.[1] Again Nehemiah confronts the nobles in charge of the workers who were doing this. He reminds them that their ancestors did the same thing and brought destruction! He commanded the gates to be shut at sundown and posted a guard. The next morning, he found that the sellers had spent the night outside the gates with their goods, ready

---

[1] This problem was not new, and would not end here. See Amos 8:5 and Jer 17:19–27 for the same problems. Jesus driving the sellers out of the Temple precincts was a similar problem: "do not turn my Father's house into a market" (John 2.16).

to come in and sell. He remonstrated them: if they did it again, he would physically attack them.

He told the Levites to purify themselves and guard the gates, to keep the Sabbath holy in honor of God. The passage closes with the second prayer, asking God to remember what he did, and to spare him any judgment.

Meaning

It seems the Jerusalem leaders did not expect Nehemiah to come back to Jerusalem after his first term. So the intentions of corrupt and selfish leaders caused at least some of these problems. The priests who offer sacrifices are allowed to keep some of the grain, oil, wine, meat offered for their meals, so *they* were being supported (which tells us that, at least, the sacrifices were continuing). But other Temple workers relied on donations from the people, to support them as they did God's work. All of this is spelled out in the Law. The contributions were no longer being given, and maybe some *were* being given, but leaders were taking them for their own enrichment.

Nehemiah offers one of the many "remember" prayers in the book. This prayer contains the idea that God keeps a "record book" of the actions of people. (The passage does not indicate whether this record is for everyone or just those specially chosen by God to do his work?) Nehemiah's petition is that his "good deeds" will not be erased by the failures in his absence.

The second problem involved both Jews and Gentiles. Jewish farmers were bringing their goods into the city on the Sabbath, and the Tyrians (Phoenicians) were selling fish and other items (known for their commerce and trading networks). Nehemiah needed to forbid both groups because trading in Jerusalem on the Sabbath defeated the purpose of the day—even if it was by Gentiles who were not under the Law. (Notice that when Nehemiah discovers this violation, he waits until after the Sabbath to confront the leaders—otherwise he would violate the Sabbath, too!)

When the sellers found a way around Nehemiah's prohibition by camping overnight outside the closed gate, he threatened them: they were no longer being lazy or ignorant, they were attempting to flout God's laws with intent.

Again, Nehemiah closes with a "remember" prayer. The phrasing of the last part ("spare me…") is merely a different way of asking God not to let his good deeds be erased, as in the first prayer.

The book of Nehemiah does not close with a happy ending of blessings, joy, thanksgiving, and praise. Sadly, the history of God's people is replete with repetitive failure, selfishness, forgetfulness, and even corruption. Spiritual leaders bear responsibility for this, but in our modern age of the church, each one of us bears the responsibility of being faithful—even if our leaders are leading us astray on purpose or out of ignorance.

Application

This passage (and the ones in the next chapter) might make us wonder if Nehemiah was being too harsh. We'll discuss this more fully in the next chapter where the issue is more emphatic. Here, it it enough to say that God has told his people the best way to live. While there are practices that are not as crucial as others, the issues in this passage were the same ones that led to such unfaithfulness that it led to destruction and captivity.

Nehemiah's "remember" prayers are unique. How might we adopt them for our own use?

First, the issue behind the prayers had to do with Nehemiah's work for God and God's people. Nehemiah asked God to remember his work *because* he had worked so hard, despite the failures after he left. If we have done "good works" for God and his people, we can pray the same prayer. If not, this is a call for us to confess we have not done enough, and a petition to help us do so, so that we can offer this prayer in the future.

Second, the prayers show that God does pay attention to what we do, and that we are allowed to remind him! That might seem selfish: "remember me!" "Bless me!" But if I seek to be God's person in everything I do, then this sort of relationship and conversation is appropriate. Even if my hard work has been corrupted or stained by others, I can still ask to be remembered by God for our efforts. It is the *attitude* by which we offer ourselves that matters, not the results—because often we have no control over the full results because of outside forces. A prayer asking God to remember you and your work is appropriate—no matter how small or how successful that work has turned out to be.

Prayers for a Distinctive Faith and Life (Neh 13.25, 28-31)

And I contended with them and cursed them and beat some of them and pulled out their hair; and I made them take an oath in the name of God, saying, "You shall not give your daughters to their sons, or take their daughters for your sons or for yourselves.

And one of the sons of Jehoiada, son of the high priest Eliashib, was the son-in-law of Sanballat the Horonite; I chased him away from me. Remember them, O my God, because they have defiled the priesthood, the covenant of the priests and the Levites.

Thus I cleansed them from everything foreign, and I established the duties of the priests and Levites, each in his work; and I provided for the wood offering, at appointed times, and for the first fruits. Remember me, O my God, for good.

It is clear from Scripture that believers are to be distinct from the world in many ways. In today's world, how can a Christian practice mercy while standing firm against a secular society? What role can prayer play?

Background

This passage and its three prayers continue the story of Nehemiah's return to Jerusalem and his discovery that some reforms were still needed. The harshness with which Nehemiah draws lines between ethnicities is troubling to many in the modern world. Placing it in its proper context helps to understand it better.

Remember that the Jews had been taken into Exile mainly because they forgot who they were. They had ceased practicing and acting like God's people and were heavily influenced by other religions—gods and goddesses who did not deliver them from Egypt, protect them in the desert, or help them grow into a nation. Part of Nehemiah's task was to restore the distinctiveness and focus of the Jewish people.

In the last passage, he dealt with some reforms of the Temple and its services. Here, it has to do with marriages to foreigners (both the common people and even a priest) that were causing the people to lose their identity. Some of their children could not even read or speak their own language, but the language of foreign pagans.

This seems to have been a quite small group of people, but Nehemiah is outraged because this goes to the heart of what caused the Exile in the first place—Jews acting, thinking, and living no different than the other nations.

In the first instance, Nehemiah requires them to take an oath (a prayer vow) that they will not allow their daughters and sons to intermarry. They were apparently not capable of bringing foreigners into *their* faith but were susceptible to outside influences.

The second and third prayer have to do with the marriage of a priest to a foreigner. Unlike the other group, where it was merely a bad idea, priests were forbidden to marry anyone outside the community. This seems to have been a particular problem with one couple, as no one else is punished. This was the grandson of the high priest. Nehemiah sent him away, and the narrative ends with one of Nehemiah's "Remember" prayers, though this one, like the one in 6.14, is a negative prayer: "Remember them, O my God, because they have defiled the priesthood."

The last prayer is part of the summary of the entire book, and fitting ends with the previous "Remember" prayer. Nehemiah summarizes his worth of reforming and establishing the community and the Temple, and asks God to remember all the good he did.

Meaning

As noted above, the theme of this passage is that believers should maintain a distinct identity from others in the world. People should be able to tell that Jews (and Christians) are different in the way they live, treat others, and practice their faith. External pressures had become too strong for them, and they began to look and act like everyone else.

The ability to speak and read Hebrew would have been quite valuable to a religion that focused on scripture, prayer, worship, and the stories of their ancestors. How would they learn and worship together?

Perhaps the fierce reaction by Nehemiah is his initial reaction, and the beating and hair-pulling may not atoll have been a fight, but a formal process (like lashing) and removal of hair signified shame.[1] The fact that Nehemiah thinks a prayer vow is enough to address the problem shows that it was not widespread and did not require further actions.

The second situation has to do with a priest, and, as noted above, only involved one married couple. But it seems to have been part of the overall lack of strict focus, combined the reforms needed in 13.25-31 in the previous chapter. Leviticus 21.13-15 specifies that a high priest should not marry a Gentile, because it would defile the priesthood. Therefore, they had to be sent away.

The final "remember" prayer does not include further information or comment—just "Remember me, O my God, for good." This is probably because it stands as the final line and the closing prayer of the entire book.

Application

The modern Christian lives in a much different situation than those ancient Jews. In the West, we live in a secular country, not a theocracy. We have no central Temple, no religious governmental leaders. Our churches are

---

[1] See 2 Sam 10:4.

Prayers for a Distinctive Faith and Life (Neh 13.25, 28-31)

primarily autonomous communities of people living within a secular culture.

But the principles still stand and are ripe for prayer.

1. Our leaders need to be strong and understand what it means to lead a community. We can pray for them.

2. In a secular society, the need for accountability and stringent distinctiveness is crucial. A community of believers surrounded by a secular world will be easily influenced in all sorts of subtle ways. We can pray that God helps us discern the difference between living in the world and becoming like the world.

3. Yet none of the above means we need to adopt the same restrictions as Nehemiah without understanding the culture. In that world, Sabbath observance, preserving the ethnicity of the people (especially leaders), physical religion life, were all part of their identity. Modern Christian identity is different: we are called to service, sacrifice, and dedication to God. Our distinctiveness is seen in our attitude and actions rather than our observance of days, rituals, or who we marry. We should demonstrate forgiveness in a world that does not forgive, sacrifice in a world that seeks material goods, and humility in a world that seeks fame and status. We can pray that we exhibit those tendencies so that people see us and say, "there is something different about that person."

4. It is not always easy for a believer to know when to stand firm and condemn behaviors or attitudes. It's often easy to say, "I'm not going to be critical or judge anyone—that will be my witness in the world." Yet Jesus practiced both extreme mercy and firm judgment, knowing when each one was called for. We are to be salt *and* light.[2] We should pray for the same disinterment for ourselves.

Consider these four elemental principles from Nehemiah and his prayers. How can you incorporate them into your prayers? How can you use both a prayer-vow and a petition?

---

[2] See Matthew 5.13 and 5.14.

Summary of the Prayers in Nehemiah

The books of Ezra and Nehemiah both focus on the Jews' return from Exile and the rebuilding of the Temple and the city. In Nehemiah, the story centers on rebuilding the city wall and a renewal of faithful practice. As such, we find the theme of "remembrance," "identity," "loyalty to God," "confidence in God," and rules for living as a person of God. All of these themes, of course, are found in the seventeen prayers passage, too.

The types of prayer contain seven of the types. While most of the prayers we have studied only include one type per prayer, in Nehemiah, seven of the passages contain two or more types.

The most common types are intercessions and praises, perhaps not a surprise from the book where people seek God's help in restoration and He fulfills their petitions. There are nine petitions (1.5-11; 2.4; 4.4-5; 4.9; 5.12-13; 5.19; 6.9, 14; 13.14, 22; 13.25, 28-31) and seven praise-prayers (1.5-11; 9.6-11; 9.12-25; 9.26-31; 9.32-37; 12.24; 12.27, 31, 42, 46).

The rest of the prayers are two each of confessions (1.5-11; 9.6-11), curses (4.4-5, 5.12-13), vows (5.12-13, 13.25, 28-31), thanksgiving (12.24; 12.27, 31, 42, 46), and blessing (8.6; 9.3-5).

Application

It should not be surprising that, in a story of difficulty and accomplishment of God's people, we find so much variety in prayer. Part of this is also due to the charter of Nehemiah: faithful, strong, and subservient to God.

Prayers of Praise

We studied seven praise prayers in Nehemiah, though four of those were part of one long prayer praising God for all he has done for the Jews in the past and the present (9.6-11, 12-25, 26-31, 32-37). These four give us a wonderful structure to use for our own prayers (). More importantly, perhaps, is what they teach us about praise. It is often the case that we do not know how to offer prayers of praise. We might say that we praise God for his love and goodness, for his mercy, for creation…and then might find outsells at a loss. But this long prayer shows us what a detailed and deep praise-prayer can sound like. Certainly, we praise him for being the Creator, for acting in history, and for being our savior. We can recall times in the past when God has been gracious, as well as current graciousness. The unique element in this long prayer is that it shows us the connection between confession and praise: we can praise him *because* he hears our confessions and forgives—that is the sort of God he is.

The other three praise prayers remind us that any type of prayer can begin with praise as an introduction (1.5-11), that creativity can be part of prayer (12.24), and that physical acts are also part of prayer (12.27, 31, 42, 46).

Prayers of Thanksgiving

Thanksgiving and praise are intimately connected. We might think of praise as the broader subject that focused on God and his character, while thanksgivings focus on what He has done for us individually. In Nehemiah, both of the thanksgivings are connected with prayers of praise (12.24; 12.27, 31, 42, 46).

Petitions

There are more prayers of petition in Nehemiah that any other type. This is not surprising since the book is about facing adversity from within and without while trying to seek God's will to rebuild Jerusalem and the faith.

All the prayers which ask God for something in Nehemiah are petitions—there are no intercessions. This may be because all the Jews were in need together. Nehemiah and others did not need to pray for others, because they were all in need of the same prayers.

These prayers teach us many things about petitionary prayer:

- the connection between God's actions and our responsibilities (2.4)

- how our "passion" for something should not override our desire for God's will (4.9)

- how a physical act along with a petition is appropriate (5.12-13)
- petitions can address the past as well as the present (5.19)
- that petitionary prayer can be part of daily life (6.9, 14)
- From Nehemiah, we learn that a petition asking God to remember our good work is not inappropriate (13.14, 22; 13.25, 28-31).

Confession

It is not surprising that in a book which deals with the need to reform one's faith and practiced confession is found as part of the prayers. In Nehemiah, we learn that confession can be part of a flow of prayers from praise to petition to confession to praise (1.5-11; 9.6-11). This is a good way to place our prayers of confession in a context, instead of making them stand alone.

Vow

As we have noted throughout this study, prayer-vows are unusual in modern prayer. Yet they are found often in the Bible. The prayers of Nehemiah give us two examples of how prayer-vows function (5.12-13; 13.25, 28-31).

Blessings and Curses

There are two blessings and two curse-prayers in Nehemiah (though the first curse-prayer is connected with a petition). The first blessing demonstrates how we should be moved to offer blessings upon God when we hear his Word (8.6). The second is part of the long prayer in chapter 9 and gives us an excellent model for how to begin any type of prayer with a blessing as an introduction (9.3-5).

As we have discussed in previous studies, curse-prayers are difficult for us. We may often curse people—or want to curse them—but most of us probably feel that we should not ask God to curse them. The way of Jesus suggests that we should leave any desire for retribution of others to God (Matt 5.44; 18.21-22). This concept is also found in the Old Testament (Prov 25.21-22). Nehemiah wanted those who abused god's people to experience abuse—but he turned it over to God (4.4-5).

There is a second kind of curse-prayer that may make more sense to us. It is a prayer that contains a condition curse: if you don't do this, then this will happen. This is the sort of prayer we see in 5.12-13.

Summary

The book of Nehemiah, while not a long book, contains many prayers covering every prayer type except intercession and lament. These prayers serve an excellent model for enriching our own prayers.

The Book of Esther—no prayers, no mention of God!

The book of Esther is unique among all the books of the Old and New Testament—there is no mention of God and no prayers! Can we learn anything about prayer from such a book? Read on to find out.

Background

The king of Persia, Xerxes, and his wife, Queen Vashti, throw a large, week-long feast and party (the Persians were known for their extravagant feasts). The king, full of food and drink, demands his wife come to him, but she refuses. Stunned, he asks his counselors what he should do. (There is a touch of humor here: the powerful King of Persia is turned down by his wife and has to ask his political counselors how he should handle his marriage problems.) They tell him he should get rid of her and choose a new Queen from among all those in Persia.

A great beauty contest is held. Those chosen are given weeks of spa treatments and preparations. One of these girls is Esther, a Jewish woman who only has an uncle named Mordecai. Esther is the most beautiful of all and becomes the Queen of Persia.

Her uncle overhears a plot to overthrow the king. He tells Esther, who tells the king, and the men are caught and executed. But her uncle has an unrelated problem. The captain of the King's guard is Haman, a proud man. As he walks through the city gates with his entourage, he requires all to bow before him. But Mordecai will not. This infuriates Haman, and when he discovers that Mordecai is a Jew, he plots to destroy all the Jews. He asks the king to make a declaration that on such a day, all the Jews will be fair game. The king signs it.

Mordecai goes to Esther, but her problem is that even the Queen is not to appear before the king on his throne unless summoned. After fasting, she appears before him. He grants her an audience, and she begins by inviting him to a dinner with her. She wants to proceed carefully because Haman is the second-most powerful man in Persia.

That night, the king cannot sleep, and so he calls for his attendant to read from the king's records (*that would probably put anyone to sleep*). One of the passages read to him is the one about Mordecai uncovering the assassination plot. The king finds that nothing had been done for Mordecai, so he calls for Haman, and asks "What shall be done for the man whom the king wishes to honor." Haman, in all his arrogance, assumes the king means *him*. " So he tells the king:

> *"For the man whom the king wishes to honor, 8 let royal robes be brought, which the king has worn, and a horse that the king has ridden, with a royal crown on its head. 9 Let the robes and the horse be handed over to one of the king's most noble officials; let him robe the*

> *man whom the king wishes to honor, and let him conduct the man on horseback through the open square of the city, proclaiming before him: 'Thus shall it be done for the man whom the king wishes to honor.'"*

To his mortification, he tells Haman to do just that *for Mordecai*, and Haman should be the one who conducts him through the city, praising him.

But Haman was invited to the banquet between the king and Esther, assuaging his shame—but not for long. Esther tells the king of the plot to kill all the Jews—and that she is a Jew. The king, enraged, leaves the room to gather himself before deciding what to do. Haman, realizing his folly of trying to kill the Queen's people, approaches her to plead for mercy. He is too close to her as the king returns, prompting the king, as he returns, to exclaim, "Will he even assault the queen in my presence, in my own house?!" The guards take Haman away to hang him on the same gallows he had built to hang Mordecai.

The king is unable to stop the declaration of the murder of the Jews because the king's laws cannot be changed! So Esther suggests a second edict which ordered the Jews to prepare, assemble, and defend themselves. It was a great day of victory for the Jews. (There is again some bit of humor here, making fun of the idea that laws cannot be repealed, and the well-known complexity of Persian law-making).

The Jews celebrate, beginning the first celebration of an annual holiday known as Purim.

Meaning

The book of Esther was preserved because it tells of the institution of the feast of Purim. It also tells us about the difficulties Jews often faced when living under foreign governments.

Why are there no mention of God or prayer? It is likely because the authors wanted to tell a story, set in a pagan setting, where God works behind the scenes. We often have the idea that, in the Bible, God's involvement is always miraculous. Yet we know from experience that most of the time, God's actions in the world are in the everyday things of life, only visible to those with eyes of faith.

God and prayer underlie the entire story. A poor, orphaned girl become the Queen of Persia just in time to save the Jews from extinction? God and prayer were behind that. The king cannot sleep one night and just happens to read about Mordecai and decides to honor him? God and prayer were behind it. The king allows Esther to approach the throne at just the right time? God and prayer were behind it.

But there are some things in the book that are more obvious signs of God and prayer. When Mordecai tells Esther of Haman's plot, and she is worried because she would have to approach the king unbidden, Mordecai says,

> *"Do not think that in the king's palace you will escape any more than all the other Jews. For if you keep silence at such a time as this, relief*

> *and deliverance will rise for the Jews from another quarter, but you and your father's family will perish. Who knows? Perhaps you have come to royal dignity for just such a time as this."*

First, Mordecai's words that "relief and deliverance will rise for the Jews from another quarter" is an obvious reference to God's deliverance. Second, his suggestion that "Perhaps you have come to royal dignity for just such a time as this" also points to God's work.

Moreover, fasting is mentioned three times, and we know that fasting is always accompanied by prayer. When the edict of Haman goes out, the Jews fast (and pray) for deliverance. When Esther decides to go before the king, she asks Mordecai to get all the Jews in the city together to fast (and pray). Two fasts that imply prayers of petition. Finally, the feast of Purim involved fasting in celebration of God's deliverance, which would have included prayer as well.

Application

The book of Esther helps us remember that prayer, and God's answers, are not always obvious, grand, or out in public. An answer to prayer might be an every day even that most people would see as common. Or it might be a seeming "coincidence" that works out an answer to prayer.

This should not surprise us. God is not some outsider who normally breaks into the world to dazzle us with his appearance and actions. He created the world, he moves within it, and it in Him. Of course he would work through the lives, events, and world of which He is so intimately and caringly connected.

An unbeliever might say, "oh, how lucky," or "what fortune!" But the eyes of faith know it is God, working steadily in his world, for those who pray.

Appendix
Prayers by Category

The following is a list of every prayer in each of the nine categories: blessings, confession and repentance, curses, intercession, lament, petition, praise, thanksgiving, and prayer-vow. Some prayers occur in more than one category because the passage contains more than one type of prayer.

Blessings

Renewing your faith through prayer and physical acts (Neh 8.6)

How to offer a prayer of confession, Part 1 (Neh 9.3-5)

Confession and Repentance

- Prayer and Divorce? (Ezra 10.1-11)
- Pure Confession—no requests, no excuses, no reasons (Ezra 9.6-15)
- Calling and Prayer (Neh 1.5-11)
- How to offer a prayer of confession, Part 2 (Neh 9.6-11)

Curses

- Is It ever Appropriate to Ask God to Curse Someone? (Neh 4.4-5)
- Are you aware of how you treat those who are different? (Neh 5.12-13)

Intercession

- Prayer and the Surprising Acts of God (Ezra 1.3)

Lament

There are no Laments in Ezra, Nehemiah, or Esther.

Petition

- Living Faithfully Under a Non-Believing State (Ezra 6.12)
- Prayer and Fasting Go Together (Ezra 8.21)
- Calling and Prayer (Neh 1.5-11)
- Prayer and Our Responsibility to Act (Neh 2.4)
- Is It ever Appropriate to Ask God to Curse Someone? (Neh 4.4-5)
- Does your passion match God's will? (Neh 4.9)

Appendix: Prayers by Category

- Are you aware of how you treat those who are different? (Neh 5.12-13)

- Praying about your past (Neh 5.19)

- Pray Continually and Do Your Job (Neh 6.9, 14)

- Asking God to Remember You (Neh 13.14, 22)

- Prayers for a Distinctive Faith and Life (Neh 13.25, 28-31)

- The Book of Esther—no prayers, no mention of God! (Esther 4.21?)

Praise

- Patience in Prayer and the Joy of God's Answers (Ezra 3.11)

- Praying for Secular Leaders and Government (Ezra 7.27-28)

- Calling and Prayer (Neh 1.5-11)

- How to offer a prayer of confession, Part 2 (Neh 9.6-11)

- How to offer a prayer of confession, Part 3 (Neh 9.12-25)

- How to offer a prayer of confession, Part 4 (Neh 9.26-31)

- How to offer a prayer of confession, Part 5 (Neh 9.32-37)

- Bringing Together the Past and the Present in Your Prayers (Neh 12.24)
- Adding Joy and Physical Acts to Your Prayers (Neh 12.27, 31, 42, 46)

Thanksgiving

- Patience in Prayer and the Joy of God's Answers (Ezra 3.11)
- Bringing Together the Past and the Present in Your Prayers (Neh 12.24)
- Adding Joy and Physical Acts to Your Prayers (Neh 12.27, 31, 42, 46)

Prayer-Vow

- Are you aware of how you treat those who are different? (Neh 5.12-13)
- Prayers for a Distinctive Faith and Life (Neh 13.25, 28-31)

ABOUT THE AUTHOR

Markus McDowell is a writer, editor, and researcher, and has lectured at various universities in the US, Europe, and the UK. He has a Ph.D. from Fuller Theological Seminary and a law degree from the University of London, and is the author of *Prayers of Jewish Women: Studies of Patterns of Prayer in the Second Temple Period*, *Prayer in the Ancient Stoic Tradition*, and *Epistolary Prayer in the Apostolic Fathers*.

To receive notice of publication of other volumes in the *Praying Through the Bible* series, and for notification of other books and articles by Markus McDowell, join the mailing list or follow his Facebook page.

Visit the website at www.markusmcdowell.com

OTHER BOOKS BY MARKUS MCDOWELL

Nonfiction

Prayers of Jewish Women: Studies of Patterns of Prayer in the Second Temple Period
Prayer in the Ancient Stoic Tradition: With a Comparison to Prayers of the New Testament
Epistolary Prayer in the Apostolic Fathers
The Practice of Prayer: The Character of Prayer
Let the Bible Speak: A Simple, Three-Part Method for Bible Study

Fiction

To and Fro Upon the Earth: A Novel (2017)
Onesimus: A Novel of Ancient Christianity (2018)
The Sky Over Chaos: Short Stories (2019)

About the Publisher

Sulis International Press publishes fine fiction and non-fiction in a variety of genres. For more, visit the website at
https://sulisinternational.com

Subscribe to the newsletter at
https://sulisinternational.com/subscribe/

Follow on social media
https://www.facebook.com/SulisInternational
https://twitter.com/Sulis_Intl
https://www.pinterest.com/Sulis_Intl/
https://www.instagram.com/sulis_international/

www.ingramcontent.com/pod-product-compliance
Lightning Source LLC
Chambersburg PA
CBHW030053100526
44591CB00008B/127